Financial Independence

A wealth creation system for all Australians

Financial Independence - A wealth creation system for all Australians
© Bruce Shackelford

First published—August 2018
Second Edition—October 2019

 A catalogue record for this book is available from the National Library of Australia

ISBN: 978-0-6487030-0-6 (paperback)

All rights reserved. No part of this publication may be reproduced, stored in a retrieval system, transmitted in any form or by any means, electronic, mechanical, photocopying, recording or otherwise without the written permission of the copyright owner and publisher.

DEDICATION

To all the Home-Buyers that have not had a choice in the last 60 years - now there is my product which is not just a home loan but a system that is fair to all and makes people financially independent.

CONTENTS

Introduction vii

Chapter One 1
Chapter Two 43
Chapter Three 89
Chapter Four 109

Conclusion 131
Final Message 193

INTRODUCTION

I am almost 73! Having commenced at 18 I have been in the finance industry for 55 years. More than 2 life sentences! It was a different era in Banking back in the 1970's when I joined the Commonwealth Bank of Australia (CBA) in Melbourne. I started in the Commonwealth Development Bank (CDB) of Australia (now defunct) and the only thing that I remember from those days was how little I got in my pay packet. CBA makes Billions these days but I am sure employees get a bit more in their pay. Inflation has certainly had an effect and eased the problem. The CDB has some significance for me as that was the first time that I met Ron Elliott who was later promoted to CEO. He relocated to Sydney. I was honoured later when he invited me to play golf at Australia Golf Club. He was a great man in my eyes – he resigned to nurse his wife who died later of cancer.

I was happy where I was! Learning about Farm loans and driving high powered GT falcons. I was a typical young fellow, an up and coming golfer with a fascination for sport. Perhaps it was that fascination with sport or like minds or something else that just clicked when I met Geoff Heskett and later his lovely wife Val. They were to become life-long friends. He was a bit older than me but he was a clever guy and I guess we just clicked – he was my immediate boss in CDB. Most of the work was pretty mundane involving administration of farmers and their loan requirements including equipment finance. Geoff never left Melbourne due to sporting commitments. He was one of the best sports-man I have ever met. In his hay-day he played for the Australian Basketball Team. Just before I arrived he played an exhibition match against the American Globe-trotters who were themselves great entertainers at the end of their careers. Geoff was a colossus as a volley ball player and could just as easily have played for Australia in that sport. He was also an excellent tennis player and coach (in and out of CDB). **A natural sports-man but very quick witted and a real friendly guy.**

After CDB I become a Home Loan Specialist in about 7 city branches. Northcote branch was the furtherest afield – I also processed personal and vehicle loans and some hire purchase contracts. I was then transferred to Chancery House Branch in Bourke Street in the same capacity. That branch was regarded as one of CBA's most elite especially in the 70's.

A series of events surrounding the sudden death of the branch manager (Clive Mander) catapulted me into Commercial Lending i.e. loans for businesses, balance sheets, profit and loss statements, cash flow budgets and financial reports. I have written a separate chapter covering my exploits in the commercial area (chapter 4) – **it was a real journey for me. I enjoyed it immensely!** It wasn't till I was transferred to Branch Lending and saw the Administrative side that I was introduced to Foreign Currency Loans (unhedged). A very tricky facility based on an ever changing exchange rate. Back in the 70's the old Bank of NSW was shown to be totally incompetent with FCL's. The little knowledge that they had was just enough to get them into trouble. And trouble is what they caused. That bank was hated by farming communities for decades after. **That Bank is now Westpac.**

Commercial and Home Lending are what all banks do in their branches (and lots of other things including every-day and on-line banking). All of the Major Banks have branch networks all over Australia. The smaller/newer Banks have significant networks with no doubt a goal of being Australia wide. There are lots of people with that entrepreneurial flair that need start-up costs for businesses (not just equipment for doctors and dentists setting up practices). All sorts of other loan facilities including overdrafts fall under the commercial arm of a trading bank (in the Branch). One of the big problems for borrowers is the branch network itself. It is a standard bank requirement that **each** branch has to stand alone and make a profit (or risk closure). This is where "irresponsible lending" comes in. This is discussed in detail later in the book including its negative impact on the borrower.

The CBA days were probably the happiest of my life – I was still young and still believed it was all before me. Anyway my next stop was Standard Chartered Bank in the **ritzy** end of Collins Street, Melbourne (near my first Dentist). It like many other merchant banks got banking licences gratus of The Federal Government. Although that gesture would prove short-lived. In my view Standard Chartered remained a boutique lender and very different from the normal Trading Bank.

I was an un-employed credit analyst when I was head-hunted by Tony Wigginton, the Head of Lending. **I was chuffed!** Wigginton was a qualified accountant and a gifted lender with New York experience (Bankers Trust). I had a large desk overlooking The Old Melbourne Club (very toffy), 2 or 3 analysts and a portfolio of about 150 loans. One client owned a Meatworks in Deniliquin NSW – I had an enjoyable trip by light plane up and back.

Commercial Lending is the only real function of a merchant bank. I learnt a lot from Wigginton! Apart from anything else we got along well. I have generally found that all good guys in finance are good at what they do.

In the end The Federal Government was not satisfied with the additional licences and revoked them all. There was a mass exodus of staff from Standard Chartered Bank (including me). I suppose it was a sea-change as much as anything. The whole family went on a holiday to Far north Queensland to visit Linda's mom and came back through Townsville. Linda is my wife! Ultimately, we all shifted back to Townsville to live.

Linda was born in Townsville although I met her in Melbourne. We got a record price for our Melbourne house and I took a breather from finance. I bought a beautiful heritage home in North Ward with stunning water views of Magnetic Island plus a successful business.

Later, I took on a large property development and a partner which I didn't know well enough. The development was on the outskirts of Townsville with long range views of Magnetic Island (refer pages 92, 93 and part of 95 for a better explanation) – the property encompassed a massive block of land with a large hill in it, hence the name "Seaview Park". Eventually, I sold the business and repaid the bank loan and overdraft. Luckily I retained the house!

After the aforementioned property debacle I returned to finance (refer pages 93, 94 and bits of 95). I spent 5 years with Aussie Home Loans and approximately 20 to 25 years with Home Loan Connexion (HLC).

The most important thing in my life is the H/L system that I have developed. It has so many benefits (apart from acquiring the house). All Australians can have my system in lieu of a conventional H/L that has NO benefits. The system also provides a house you can keep! Fundamental to understanding this issue, is understanding that taking out a normal loan is not necessarily the answer. It may and it may not be! I have been involved with every loan known to man. Sudden job loss or illness can turn keeping the family home into a nightmare. There are no safeguards with a conventional loan. More often than not the fine print in an insurance policy will exclude a legitimate claim. You might think insurance will save me. Insurance Companies like collecting premiums and that's about all. As I speak many people in Sydney and Melbourne are losing their homes –this dreadful situation has always been a concern to me. On the news there is a shocking story of a guy that bought a house in French's Forest many years ago. He bought a house that he wanted to live in forever. **Something special that we would all want!** It cost half a million dollars after a 50% cash deposit. Unfortunately, he got seriously ill and couldn't work. He now has H/L debt of a million dollars which he can't possibly clear unless he sells (leaving him and his wife out on the street). His loan with the bank is more than 30 days in arrears. This story is typical of many in the same situation. In fact the National news has said there will be 60,000 H/L defaults in the current financial year. This is a damming statistic and one that I think will open up mortgage lenders and banks to ridicule i.e. they are financing a portion of family homes that will be lost down the track. **With my H/L system the aforementioned situation would not exist – eliminating mortgage stress is a cornerstone of my system.**

You might get there with a whole series of loans but the odds are stacked heavily against you. Good luck runs out! There are many factors that determine success i.e. what cash equity you had in the first place, what business purchase was involved (or it may just have been a start-up of your own), did you have prior knowledge and expertise as opposed to wildly having a go, how did you get started, when was the initial success (or failure) and was the whole process delayed. Why?

Financial Independence is illusive! I can categorically say that it is not easily achieved with a conventional loan or series of loans. It involves a lot more.

Three decades ago I had a strong conviction that the H/L borrower was getting a raw deal – the risk of loss was high and was always there. I therefore designed a system around the same approval process. It had to avoid all the pitfalls, get the H/L credit and satisfy all the other criteria of a H/L application.

Hence the borrower gets the H/L of say $400,000 plus the following benefits:

- Removal of mortgage stress forever!
- A set up that outstrips any conventional loan in the country.
- 100% borrower control (at present control is 100% to the lender/bank).

- Great access to cash – your own and other.
- Retire H/L debt easily in 5 to 10 years – this is your decision (currently 3 decades with a conventional loan if you are lucky).
- Pay cash for cars and drive new cars every 4 years.
- Invest in property before and after retirement.
- Multiply your superannuation benefit 3 or 4 times – at present everybody is chasing a better interest return. Which fund is the best? They are all up and down!
- Business operators can use turnover to reduce the personal H/L interest that they pay.

These are only half of the benefits! Change your life for the better! Be part of the ground swell that wants and gets more in their H/L – a totally new deal.

I am giving Seminars in Townsville and Northern Queensland. God willing these will extend all over the country.

A Major bank has blamed the borrower for the increase in H/L defaults. The other Majors accepted this because defaults are spread **evenly** between all of them (not because they like each other).

Unfortunately, Major Banks influence the market more than anybody else. According to the News they enjoy 85% of the financial market. Based on increasing defaults they then made loans harder to get. And because the Major Banks acted together a Credit Squeeze occurred – a mother of a Credit Squeeze. House prices plummeted worse than ever before. I remember when H/L interest rates soared beyond 15% per annum and the value of residential houses fell dramatically. Well the effect of the latest Credit Squeeze **was much worse.**

The default statistics that I have are only for Sydney and Melbourne. What about the rest of Australia? Some folks are looking at negative equity (as a direct result of falling house prices and actions of the Major Banks). An earlier report by Alan Kohler of the ABC News put negative equity in Tasmania at a record high of 27% i.e. more than 1 in 4 of all owners where the mortgage was greater than the value of their property. Thank goodness the position has eased somewhat with loans now easier to get once again. However, we are not out of the woods yet! The economy (and that of the World) is somewhat delicately placed at the moment with US/China trade wars and low wages growth. Australia could still find itself in a recession. Let's hope not!

I believe the borrower was never the problem. Default and loss under any loan let alone a H/L is a complex issue that is discussed at length in this book. The borrower was accused of understating living expenses. How convenient! And a good way of blaming the borrower. A Major Bank is not going to accuse itself. **Overall, I find it very strange, I use exactly the same process in getting my H/L system approved. I haven't had a default or sell up in 30 years.** The problem is in fact the H/L that the Major Banks and everybody else is shovelling out to the Australian public. **There is absolutely no protection for a borrower with the current H/L i.e. sudden job loss, one income lost, overcommitted due to a life event, illness or simply something totally unexpected can put a borrower in default.** Irrespective of how living expenses are assessed more often than not the most marginal borrower is the best at paying back the loan.

I would like to share some of my experiences as a finance broker that has lost everything due to a dishonest brother, a criminal Major Bank and the GFC. I appreciate fully what was done to me, and this may help others avoid the same pitfalls.

I had a large property subdivision on the outskirts of Townsville. A partner too! There was a large commercial loan in the name of Frost Industries Ltd and a working overdraft in the name of Pacific Property Pty Ltd – my wife and I signed guarantees to link us to the aforementioned facilities at the outset. Unbeknown to me the Branch Manager called Linda in to sign a guarantee that they had over looked at the outset. Taking a guarantee after the event is against the law. My wife and I will sign a statutory declaration to this effect. This is akin to some dishonest bank employee forging the signature on a mortgage to protect themselves.

Major Banks employ a lot of people and do a lot of good things in the community. They also employ unscrupulous individuals that will do anything to protect themselves. Major Banks make Billions! Some of this should be sacrificed to expose criminal activity. Of course there is always the difficulty of catching them in the act. All those old bank files are locked away! Imagine all the mischief and dishonesty they would disclose.

What I have disclosed is criminal activity. On The 7.30 Report (ABC) the Deputy Prime-minister has said that nobody trusts the Major Banks. That might be so but they make up the very fabric of our society and people always need to borrow. It's how they do it that matters! (see comments later in this introduction). The National news has said that The Major Banks account for 85% of the commercial and home loan market (a power-full grip). Whilst brokers account for more than 50% of all H/L's written, many of them are for Major Banks via Aggregation Companies. Major Banks also have their own mobile lenders handling their commercial and home loan requirements. Major Bank branches also write H/L's.

Overall Major Banks have a stranglehold on the market (this is not the issue). My system is just a clever way of using what is available – skip to the end of this introduction to read all about it.

Years of experience with financial institutions has given me a greater insight into their workings than the average person. How they skinned me and I'm sure every other Australian that has endured the "mortgagee process" is really quite simple. It's ugly too!

My wife and I owned a two storey penthouse on top of a Four Star Hotel. There was an adjoining 18 hole golf course (probably why I bought it). First, my brother double crossed me and the GFC followed –

without the GFC I would have survived. I couldn't sell anything.

I got all the sell up figures from the newspaper – I never trusted the bank. Based on the low selling price of the penthouse and what was owing on the loans and credit cards I estimated there was a surplus of close to $100,000. The lender (in this case a Major Bank) gives no account of what takes place i.e. the bank can do what it likes. The fact that there is no accounting to a mortgagee is **disgraceful**. This explains why he is ripped off every time. The Bank took possession of our unit kicked us out and then sold it. A bank is never in a hurry when selling you up – in fact it takes as long as it likes. After-all, the bank accounts to no-one except themselves and their own file! The person being sold up wants it to happen quickly so they can keep abreast of the figures and what is happening. This is impossible! The bank keeps charging interest on the loans and credit cards (like they were still being used by the borrower). How long this process goes on for cannot be determined (it can only be determined by the bank and happens according to its overall plan for each individual borrower). Remember, the bank does not have to account to anybody.

I only became aware of this unconscionable behaviour by a Major Bank when it happened to me and my wife. I have no doubts that all H/L Lenders do exactly the same thing (that doesn't make it right). I'm sure there is a clause in the mortgage protecting the bank.

The bank's representative said that all the credit card debt would be included with the home loan. **What a dreadful lie!** You are undoubtedly more vulnerable when you are being sold up than at any other time. It doesn't say a lot for human beings. **Man's inhumanity to man!** I believe our Major Bank wrote the book on the subject. The credit cards were left open. And after finalising interest to date sold to a collection agency. The agency left me alone, but when they started harassing Linda I stepped in and wrote to the Major Bank C/O Alexandria at the collection agency who forwarded it on to the Bank.

I know the Bank received it because the harassment stopped! We had nothing anyway thanks to them.

My Bank was a Major Bank with no constraints on it whatsoever. When I look back on everything. What a con! The Bank guys were all lies and bad behaviour – they were also smarmy like used car salesman. I honestly thought they were doing Linda and I a favour at the time. What humbug! They were just glib liars!

Please also remember that any shortfall is picked up by a mortgage Insurer. The Major Bank never loses, only the insurer. If the shortfall is large or if the insurer doesn't like you for some reason he can bankrupt you. In this country there is a real stigma attached to bankruptcy that is difficult to overcome.

However, the lack of any accountability by the Lender is the main stumbling block in what is a very dishonest system.

The Major Bank involved in selling up our penthouse was the same organisation guilty of all the lies and deception. The Bank will have a hard time refuting a statutory declaration when their only evidence is a Bank file that confirms what I have said happened. What was said to us at the time regarding amalgamation of home loan and credit card debt was very important to us. We were relying on their honesty. What a joke! Their actions were all the more despicable considering I had sold my trail book for $46,000 (well below its real value) so that $51,000 in body corporate debt could be paid i.e. their debt would have been $51,000 higher (this was done so we would owe less to the bank). What a joke! And certainly never acknowledged by the bank so in so's. I should have kept the money for Linda and I, not those bank shysters. I thought I was doing the right thing. What a fool I was (but not dishonest like them).

A court order on the Bank file would be required to disclose their dirty sell up tactics (and that will never happen). I believe the Major Bank can be brought to account on these two issues (indented above), and they can be shamed on sell up procedures as no evidence to refute can be produced. The Bank's file would only shoot them in the foot.

I owe The Major Bank in question big-time and might catch up with them on a TV Programme I know – I might even get restitution. They make billions flogging ordinary people and deserve a bit of pay back (they can certainly afford it). They also deserve the spotlight being shone on some of their activities. Some are unacceptable and some are definitely un-Australian.

It has been difficult attempting a recovery in the finance industry (almost impossible). Going under financially due to the combined effects of my brother and the GFC were pretty unfair. My only sin with my brother (now deceased) was generosity and being a bit stupid. I have been shunned in the finance industry because of it.

Actually what's happened to me is a very poor reflection on those that I have encountered in finance. My brother was living like a dog so I bought him a car and helped him reunite with his 3 kids. The fourth was a female already married. I went down because he took all my liquidity. For my trouble, I have been ostracized in the finance industry. I had all the qualifications and something really special that I will talk about shortly. I have lurched from one Loan Aggregator to another – probably written three loans in the past 10 years. If you don't have a brokerage and don't have a Loan Aggregator you don't have a job. And if you can't place a loan you haven't got a job. That was me! I have run into 30 or 40 ratbags that couldn't care less if I had a job. Finance is all I knew (all my qualifications were in finance). I am talking about bosses of Aggregation companies, a number of on-line Aggregators, State Managers and several individual brokers all with no integrity. It is difficult submitting loans through another broker. You have to rely on them sticking to a deal. I've found one person that I knew 20 years ago but that is difficult anyway.

I am optimistic about the future of the H/L industry. Everybody else will be also when they access my H/L system. It gives all borrowers a fair deal! The current H/L is not fair! Or not fair enough! The level of risk to the borrower is too high at present. The current H/L is the problem (and it needs to be replaced).

I am quite prepared to forget about the Major Bank's dishonest selling practices. My H/L system will be adopted **universally** and they will disappear. The reported 60,000 defaults in Sydney and Melbourne will then reduce to virtually NIL. Home lenders/Banks will then only resort to sell up tactics when there is no alternative i.e. a breach of the Credit Code or some criminal activity like money laundering or a borrower that over steps the mark. Loan default is still possible with my system! The total number would probably be less than 50. Lack of accountability in respect of Home or commercial loan sell ups would no longer be a concern because of the aforementioned low figure quoted.

The Major Banks (and other banks) as well as other Retail Home Lenders provide all **the machinery for my H/L system.** The Major Banks are all listed on the Stock Exchange. Their real owners are shareholders! The Major Banks do a lot of good things in the community and will always need to chase profits to appease shareholders. It serves no purpose to continually rail against Banks generally. They might be a bit shabby with issues of social conscience. **However, we are a capitalist society after all,** and financial institutions attend Royal Commission's from time to time (and checks and balances are put in place).

When you go to the Supermarket you only select what you want. It is the same process for me as a finance broker. I select what is most beneficial to the borrower. **The machinery for my H/L system** is with Financial institutions that you and I deal with every day.

When Home lenders and Banks adopt my system their standing in the community will improve. The reason is simple the borrower will borrow a lot more in a safer environment. And the Lender or bank will earn a lot more! Lending institutions will have to give up control but the incentive will be there i.e. **a large perhaps massive increase in revenue.**

This is the introduction to a spectacular system. I hope you enjoy the rest of the book!

Chapter One

I recently wrote and had published a book called *"Wealth Creation - My Life in Finance and Golf"*. This book was criticised for its personal content and life experiences. Obviously, readers are not generally interested in somebody else's experiences, for as riveting as they maybe they are not their own. Whilst refuting some aspects of this criticism, I have taken it on board I guess as this book relates to finance and a unique financial product that was discussed in the final chapter of my original book. In any event I believe the original book had considerable merit - it is in 50 libraries up the East coast of Australia including The National Library of Australia in Canberra (ACT). I have also received a personal commendation from the Prime Minister regarding the book. I think that it is fair to say that both major parties want to see ordinary Australians better off (and that is what this Book is all about).

In my mind the underlying reason for writing the original book was the unique home loan product that is in the final chapter of that book. I have always believed that my product should be universally available to the man in the street i.e. **a product** that is "tried and true" allowing borrowers to make money, run their own show (no bank manager) and own their own home a lot quicker than is currently possible (plus many other benefits).

None of these benefits exist in conventional loans advanced by banks and non-bank lenders all over the country in recent decades.

The 1st edition of my first book was published in 2015 (80 pages). I must have been a little dissatisfied with the end result so my life-long fascination with sport prevailed with the next edition. A further 40 pages was added covering both Footy codes i.e. AFL and NRL and a few other sports in the 2015 sporting calender. It was a detailed account of all the players and the teams that I thought were in contention. It was also a comprehensive effort on my part as a lover of sport and more particularly as a fan.

Just like every other fan I have had my allegiance's and opinions on what would or should be the outcome. In AFL I have always barracked for the Richmond Football

Club with a fondness for Hawthorn (HFC). My wife and youngest son barrack for Hawthorn and they have had a string of successes in recent years. In 2018 it is in the top eight but not going as well as Richmond which is on top of the ladder. Richmond also won the AFL Premiership in 2017. The standout player for me and other supporters is Dusty Martin – he has got all the accolades, winning the coveted Brownlow Medal, in the same year as Richmond (alias The Tigers) won the Premiership. He would also be regarded by most as the best player in AFL at the moment. I was living in Melbourne 37 years ago and actually attended their last Grand Final win in 1980 – I am a bit fuzzy on who their opponents were but think it might have been their bitter rival Collingwood (the Magpies). Collingwood has a few other nicknames. Unfortunately, the only one that comes to mind is a bit derisive i.e. Colli-wobbles.

My eldest son Stephen is a fanatical supporter of The Tigers and often gets a plane to Melbourne to see the match. This particular incident is both priceless and hilarious and relates to umpire bashing. All part of the sport! Last year he went with one of his footy mates – it was at the MCG. Anyway there was a free kick given against The Tigers near where they were sitting. There was a derisive howl from Tiger supporters who obviously didn't agree with the decision. Anyway the umpire in question "Ray" a senior in the umpire ranks, made the call. Stephen's mate stood up unannounced, and yelled out in a loud booming voice "Ray, it's your time to shine". Well everybody heard it including Ray who amazingly remained relatively nonplussed. The crowd went wild and almost bought the Grandstand down with laughter. It sounded hilarious and wish I had been there.

In the NRL I follow the NQ Cowboys quite religiously. At the same time I have a bit of a soft spot for The Brisbane Bronco's. They are the other Queensland team. Traditionally, The Bronco's have a lot of player's that make it into the State of Origin team (for Qld). I believe that most people regard State of Origin footy as the pinnacle of the NRL game in this country – it certainly attracts all the elite players. Petro Civoniceva, Alan Langer, Wally Lewis (the King), Darren Lockyer and Gorden Tallis and the Walters Brothers were all Broncos (now retired) and all legends of the game. Still playing for the Broncos, of course is the great Sam Thaiday and Darius Boyd.

In 2015 the giants of the game were in fact the two Queensland teams who were contesting the NRL premiership at Suncorp Stadium. It was a hum-dinger of a match! In fact I think it was the most nail-biting one I have ever seen – I also believe the sportsmanship between the two clubs was unrivalled. In the end, the match went into overtime and The Cowboys won by one point (Golden Point). If it had been a boxing match only a split decision would have appeased the crowd. Johnathon Thurston's performance was legendary – the final kick was his bit of magic. He will retire shortly but will always be remembered as one of the greats of the sport. I am not sure how The Bronco's are going this year but The Cowboys would not be happy. As a fan I have watched a lot of their games and believe the players have really put in this season. Many times The Cowboys have lost by the smallest of margins. Sporting results can be elusive no matter what you do.

I am also a Rugby Union fan. The Wallabies have been in the doldrums but a comeback is on the cards. They are just as good as the NZ Blacks and certainly have the ability to be the World's best again.

The World Cup loss in Soccer was heart breaking for Australia and Tim Cahill – he has been an absolute champion in that sport.

I watched the Wimbledon Final in both men and women – both were amazing performances. I am a Federer fan but must acknowledge that the Serbian is an exceptional athlete. A prerequisite if you aspire to be the best.

A little known Australian tennis player, John Millman recently competed in the US Open Finals. He beat the World number 2 Roger Federer and one of the all-time greats of the sport. John subsequently lost to the Serbian but gave a creditable account of himself anyway. I believe Djokovic will soon reclaim his ranking of number 1 in the World of tennis. Djokovic is clearly a passionate person and his journey back has been marred by injury.

There have been numerous giant killing efforts in most sports – this time its tennis. I believe Millman's performance is truly remarkable and a bit different in his case. He obviously has a real passion for the game including a burning desire to compete and improve that belies his ranking (in the top 100 in the World). I have seen him play on TV on a number of occasions and in particular recall his performance in Melbourne at the Rod Laver Stadium (himself one of the greatest Tennis players of all time). John is never any different and is always formidable – it's his attitude (bad shots or near misses never seem to worry him). From memory he was only just beaten in the Australian Open by a top World ranking player.

The fact that he has spent so much time on the sidelines with injury is a tribute to a great personal constitution.

In my mind Millman encaptulates the great spirit of Napolean Hill of the last century. He was the best-selling author of "Think and Grow Rich". Hill's work was sensational in the USA and it was a great motivator of men. Hill spoke of many things including ability , grit and a never give up attitude that has always been amongst the secrets of success. I believe Millman will get there. In my mind he is a champion already! There is another up and coming young fellow Alex De Minaur (please forgive me for the spelling if wrong) who has exhibited similar qualities (gives everything his best shot and hates losing).

I have always believed that Tiger Woods would return to his best in golf – with his recent second at Augusta (US Masters) there is no doubt that this has happened. He has had a remarkable career and his return to the World stage is all the more remarkable following back surgery (a prior no. 1 World ranking).

Sport and all the outcomes are really fickle but without doubt the uncertainty makes it all the more fascinating – sport has always brought different cultures and nations together and that has got to be a good thing.

I have been in finance 50+ years. I was the Senior Loans Officer in a busy CBA branch in Bourke St. Melbourne many years ago. I was also a home loan specialist and had extensive training in Commercial Finance. I have also held an Australian Credit Licence with the Australian Securities and Investment Commission (ASIC) since inception - a licencing scheme covering all finance professionals in this country.

Getting back to the original book for a minute - it was really a sports book with a financial thread. I still believe that all Australians enjoy reading about sport. The book depicted the historical premiership win of The Hawthorn Football Club (three in a row) in the AFL and the fairy-tale premiership win of the North Qld Cowboys in the NRL in the 2015 sporting season.

As a young-man and sportsman I was fortunate to have won a few golf championships at Riversdale Golf Club and the Kew Open in Melbourne. My good friend from Riversdale Golf Club, Geoffrey Sowden was also the best amateur golfer that I ever saw (in my opinion he should have turned professional). Later via mentors I was also lucky to get a birth in The Australian Amateur Championships at Victoria Golf Club (one of the best sand-belt courses around). From memory I was a bit nervous and didn't play too well.

After leaving school via my Father I had the pleasure of playing golf with the great Harry Hattersley. Harry and my Father were good friends. My Father met Harry through his job as General Manager of the Allied Mills Group in Sydney in the 1960/70's - apart from anything else I am talking about two highly intelligent individuals. I suppose the golf was one of the catalysts for the friendship i.e. they both played the sport. My father battled with the game (better than a hacker though) however Harry was an outstanding golfer. He won the Amateur Championship of Australia twice (20 years apart).

What I have in finance is ground-breaking. I have a wealth producing home loan that should be available to the man in the street- it is light years in front of any conventional loan currently available in Australia. There are a multitude of different residential housing lenders around including the Big 4 Banks - they are literally everywhere. Apart from a little tweaking (that all lenders do to differentiate their loan offering) the conventional loan has not altered in the last forty to fifty years.

I will be doing everything possible to ensure this eBook (and book) go Australia wide. A conventional loan is an inflexible product. **It gets the house and that is all - it has no other benefits and the borrower is saddled with loan repayment over three decades. My system home loan gives great access to cash and clearance of home loan debt in a fraction of the time that it takes with other home loans. It also provides a full list of benefits none of which are present in a conventional loan (refer middle chapter of this eBook or book). My system leads to financial independence and we all crave that.**

My system does not disturb any existing investment. It's just the best method of investing going forward. This system of mine sets up the machinery for future investment. Later, in my concluding remarks I will talk a lot more about having the right set-up (machinery) to invest properly without being bitten by the bad investment. Let me say quite categorically that anybody can make a bad investment. **Any-body!** The essential thing is that the bad investment must be isolated from everything else otherwise you can literally lose the lot. If you happen to purchase the so-called bad investment property using equity in the family home, then you could be in all sorts of strife. If you used the local bank manager or any number of other avenues available, I can assure you that the bad property investment is not isolated. Assuming the local bank financed your family home then I am sure you won't be able to sell the investment property even if you want to. The "all monies" clause in the original mortgage will intrude and prevent any sale. If you can meet the loss in cash, then you might be alright and retain the family home. If the value of the family home has fallen since you acquired the investment property, which has also fallen then you could be in a world of hurt. You're not so friendly bank manager will then be making all the decisions. Not you!

I will briefly discuss irresponsible lending because it is a big factor in all scenarios. If you get additional funding for investment from the same source (and this can be from your local and very friendly bank manager) the thing that automatically happens is cross collateralising (linking) of securities. This means you can't do anything without the banks approval. Look the bank manager would really be trying to help but in a default or possible default situation the friendly bank manager won't have a job if he tries to countermand any bank decision. At the end of the day if the overall situation turns ugly the bank has its mortgage to fall back on. The standard mortgage has some very nasty clauses i.e. it's a legal document prepared for the lenders protection. Mortgage clauses and their possible effects are discussed in more depth a little further on.

Irresponsible lending is a difficult and complex issue. What is irresponsible? The local bank manager is tasked with building up the branch and all its business including approval of housing loans (owner occupied or investment). Using the scenario where the borrower initially had sufficient equity for an investment purchase. The thing to remember is that the friendly bank manager gets a lot more written data about your intended investment purchase than you do. Assume we are talking about a local resort that the bank might also be trying to promote. The bank manager might have access to background information on how the resort is travelling. The valuation report would undoubtedly make comment on the resort. With the purchase of an allotment for say $150,000 the valuer may qualify his valuation at P/P by tying it to the continued viability of the resort. The borrower pays for the valuation but is not privy to its contents. Your friendly bank manager wants to put on more investment loans, so he says "yes" and in any event saying "no" is unpopular and would have to be justified. When the bank manager finances the transaction, he does so in the knowledge that you have to pay back the loan. Not him! So, the purchase goes ahead - needless to say when the block is worth $75,000 there is little you can do about it but hang on. If you earn lots of money that might get you out of trouble in due course or in the longer term the resort may come good. For most of us the outcome would be anything but rosy.

I believe irresponsible lending is involved in the above scenario. Remember to get all the information you can on any intended property purchase as the decision to proceed or let it go is yours and yours alone. Probably the most important advice is to forget what the friendly bank manager says as he is undoubtedly wearing two hats.

With my system home loan all investment transactions are **isolated**. You are the decision maker and not the local bank manager.

Please do not confuse my home loan system with investing generally. The latter activity concerns what you do with spare cash. My system relates to one of the biggest transactions you will ever contemplate i.e. buying your own residential home to live in - home ownership is sacrosanct in this country. It has always been so and continuation along the same lines is as important now as it ever was. Investing is quite separate - extreme caution needs to be exercised when investing hard earned dollars. There are a million pouncy schemes designed to catch the unsuspecting and take their cash and superannuation. Every second conman is on a TV news program for losing somebody else's life savings and walking away scot free. The so-called investment advisers have included Financial Planners, some Accountants and other un-qualified conmen. Obviously, the expertise is necessary, but **honesty is essential**. There are some very good Financial Planners around but there are also some shyster's in their ranks. Buying a house through a home lender is an entirely different thing - it is a life-long commitment secured by a first mortgage. This is negotiated through a bank or non-bank lender. My financial product is also a home loan but many times better and far more flexible by design.

Whilst my wealth creating home loan is a function of a loan facility and all about becoming financially independent, it is distinctly different from **"Investing"** as an activity. My product is all about making money out of your own residential home while you live in it – changing the landscape so the borrower has an even playing field with the lender, retiring home loan debt in record time and adding a whole range of life-style features to improve the lot of the home owner/buyer. To say this in another way, my product is really just the most advantageous way of acquiring a house. The current loan offering isn't.

I believe that a recently released book "The Barefoot Investor" provides an excellent framework for investment. How to manage your investments! Who to place your superannuation with and how to ensure that it is worth a lot more nearing retirement: the wonders of compound interest and how to use it to your benefit . How to keep ahead of inflation (the author believes that the stock market is a way to do this). Some research might be necessary to identify non-speculative stocks and what to buy however I believe his reasoning is sound. Actually a friend of mine that has seen more of the book than me confirmed that the right shares are identified. Undoubtedly, there would be many other things worthy of mention. As far as I can see there is no other guide to investing to refer to – and really the whole aspect of **"Investing" is a minefield for the un-initiated. From my point of view** if you make more in superannuation, then you can automatically make more using it or part of it in my system. I have only flicked through the aforementioned book but it looks like a clever way to get ahead and avoid the bad investments that some of us make.

I always thought that it was important to avoid capital loss and the bad investment – the promise of a high or higher than normal interest return is usually the con that sucks in the starters. That promise of a good return or a margin on your capital is a common aspect of most cons i.e. the con artist is working on the greed factor.

You can make money out of my system and combine this with sound investment practice. You will have more "cash" via my system and be able to better manage your investments (including having more superannuation at your disposal).

Investing is a tricky business and lots of people have lost their life savings using the wrong "Investment". That said I believe the book referred to is an excellent guide to making the right investments.

My system home loan is NOT an investment but it is an investment in your future.

Do you own your own home? Most of us have at least thought about owning one. A high percentage of Australians purchase their own home with the assistance of a conventional home loan which they pay off over three decades - these people have accepted the current dogma i.e. re removing years off the mortgage by paying the loan fortnightly. There is a saving to be realised however those that pursue this course have little cash for anything else. By the way the weekly payment is a bit of a fallacy as the annual amount paid is greater than the amount you pay annually with a fortnightly loan payment. Again, most people cannot pay more and still have cash leftover for other things.

Of course, there are the lucky ones who get assistance from wealthy parents or simply win the Lotto themselves.

Sadly, these fairy-tale circumstances rarely occur and don't apply to most Australians who do have a mortgage.

However, there is now an alternative in my home loan system i.e. clear home loan debt in 5 years and have great access to cash.

The problem is that the public has not had any choice in the last 50 years. A conventional loan through a bank (including the Big 4) or a non-bank lender is the only product that has been available **i.e. there has been no alternative.** My home loan system is far superior as a financial product on the 2 aspects mentioned above however it needs to be universally accepted (like conventional loans are). As a mortgage broker I have processed my loan systems personally for upwards of 20 years - some outstanding results have occurred. My only goal now is ensuring that my residential home loan system is universally used and accepted (it really is so much better than what is available).

You really don't have to throw all your "cash" at a conventional mortgage. The reward for doing that is simply not there. I personally would prefer cash under the pillow and pay my mortgage monthly. At least you could handle most crises!

Across the country I think it is now acknowledged that Finance brokers process the bulk of conventional loans - I did this myself for many years. In the back of my mind, I started to think there must be a better setup for borrowers without all the pitfalls. Those starting off could not afford to have the mortgage document and its many clauses explained to them by a lawyer. They were at a disadvantage from the start, so borrowers simply jumped in and paid as much as they could. In most cases this was sufficient to avoid trouble. At the same time there was a growing list of credit impaired borrowers and a whole industry of credit impaired lenders eager to help them out at a higher rate of interest. I believe this all came about because of the conventional loan, this is an inflexible and somewhat brutal facility which fails to adequately protect a borrower in circumstances outside his control i.e. death of one borrower, sudden job loss etc. I will discuss the aspect of sudden job loss later in this section of the book. Of course, the lender that provided the original loan (a conventional loan) will notice a different job on any subsequent loan application. However, the change for the borrower (and effect on loan repayments) is not always seamless. Sometimes the change is very difficult for the borrower.

One of the major benefits of my home loan system is the eradication of **mortgage stress**. When a sole breadwinner or joint borrower (husband or wife) loses their job, the timing can be disastrous financially. A conventional loan via a bank or non-bank lender provides virtually no relief. Generally, this involves a period of hardship allowing the borrower to pay interest only for 3 months (dispensing with normal principal and interest payments) -this is followed by a period of additional repayments so that the borrower catches up on what he has missed. If you are in the wrong part of the lending cycle and your loan is not in advance you are in a world of hurt. There is literally no chance of paying interest (almost equivalent to P & I anyway). The borrower's priority would be to feed his family.

Barring family assistance, a mortgagee's sale is certainly on the cards. If the loan is insured and most of them are, the lender won't lose only you. This could land you and your family on the street without a home. In this country if there is a shortfall, after selling the family home then the mortgage insurer can bankrupt you in trying to force some sort of restitution.

When you are left with nothing it all seems a bit unfair (pointless).

An unsatisfactory outcome really! None of us are immune to misfortune. My loan system settles the transaction in the same way as a conventional loan, but all the angst is avoided. Mortgage stress and financial difficulty is also avoided.

I know I am being a bit repetitive, but I assure you it is quite deliberate. The Conventional loan has been around too long without challenge - somebody has got to stand up for something better. If there was no alternative or the alternative was more of the same and no better, I don't think I'd bother. **The fact is my home loan system incorporates a wealth creation component which kicks in after you get the house**. A conventional loan is not a wealth creation instrument. This is simply a loan to buy a residential property. The borrower puts in a deposit and a conventional loan makes up the balance of purchase money and gets the house. A Conventional loan is then just another loan repayable to the lender. Most loans are at 90% i.e. the applicants deposit is 10%. Because the deposit is small in relation to the loan the repayment to the lender is generally a long-term commitment (3 decades). A Conventional loan is simply that you get the house and then you repay the loan. It is rigid and inflexible by design - for the lenders safety and protection. The lender wants to maximise his return not yours and avoid the bad loans as much as possible i.e. arrears and sell-ups. Did you ever wonder why the loan process is so exhaustive and drawn-out?

The lender looks at everything: ability to repay, what you have purchased, exit strategies, conduct of any existing loans, your credit file etc. If you are declined I can assure you it is an embarrassing process for all concerned. Quite frankly without full investigation you should not contemplate purchasing a house especially if you know something is wrong. If you have walked away from a credit card forget about asking for a home loan.

Perhaps I have been lucky but as a practicing finance broker I never submitted a loan that wasn't subsequently approved. Really luck had nothing to do with it for I was meticulous with all the data. You had to be!

Years ago, I ran into this applicant who was a builder/carpenter who got stiffed himself for $90,000 by some organisation that went into liquidation.

He was a strange fellow who adopted the wrong approach immediately following this incident - he decided that he would pick and choose who he would pay. He had lots of unpaid bills, but his rates notice was like reading a crime novel. Writs and every conceivable default were recorded against his title - a lovely property on half an acre near the beach. It took years to get him cleaned up, but I did and eventually sent a loan application for one of my H/L systems to a Mortgage Manager (not a mainstream lender). The loan was approved. Against my advice this applicant spent $200,000 in cash on holidays, a fancy truck for all his equipment and unbeknown to me a few shipments of marijuana - he used to sell and smoke it. Anyway, this goose did everything wrong! He then rang me up asking for help. At that stage he told me that the lender had put up his rate of interest. This was a monstrous lie of omission, he had wasted $200,000 in cash and then got his loan in arrears. The lender had no option but to put his interest rate up 2% to the default rate. After speaking to the lender and confirming the real situation I simply rang back and said I could no longer assist.

Prior to meeting me this person had obviously done something right and he still had plenty of equity to get out of a tight situation, but it was not going to be with me. I was totally flattened by the bare faced lies and criminal activity that this individual was totally unrepentant for. I really don't know whether he survived. I just didn't want to be involved. I am a bit soft hearted and almost rang back because of his wife - she had no idea how secretive and stupid he had become.

I did not have to disclose information about a reckless client who happens to be the only one in 25 years that has gone astray on my H/L system. I learnt a big lesson in life with this transaction. We are not all honest and reliable. I told this guy everything to avoid disaster and he simply ignored me. I would not have needed to give him this advice if he had been normal. As it turned out I should not have let this loose cannon access my H/L system especially given his pre-disposition for self-destruction.

The big lesson for me as a young finance broker was that this guy wasn't normal (although appearing so). I knew my facility was infallible (he wasn't) - it gets normal people out of trouble. The access to cash enables investment at a level that simply cannot happen with a conventional loan. Abuse of this wonderful benefit never happens with a normal home loan borrower (and hasn't happened since). Most Australians are normal!

My home loan system can refinance **any** existing residential home loan in Australia - it can also complete the purchase of any newly constructed home (with land). There are no exceptions and the following transactions are also encompassed:

Purchase of first and subsequent family homes including investment houses anywhere in Australia. All these properties are zoned residential.

Purchase of hobby farms (lenders decide what acreages are acceptable). All these properties are in rural residential areas.

A Conventional loan caters for all the purchases, as does my home loan system only it is many times better. A normal home loan is repayable from income say $1,964.26 p.m. over three decades or slightly less. My set-up leverages the borrower's income plus income from other sources to repay home loan debt in a much shorter period. Additional leverage options exist and a very good one for those operating their own business (this relates to turnover which varies from business to business).

Many years ago, a Father sent his son to me. He was 18 at the time and when 21 he had made $1.5M using my H/L system - he was single, and I can assure you we were both working hard. I processed a low document loan via my home loan system for an artist who would never have qualified for a conventional loan or any other loan due to the intermittent nature of her income. She has done very well with no defaults.

My home loan system has many benefits. Some of the major benefits will appeal no matter who you are. We are all different and you may simply want to focus on repaying your H/L debt quickly. That's all you can do with a conventional loan. The only difference is that you can do it a lot quicker with my system. Then again you may prefer to make money in other ways. Why not do both! The important thing to realise is you can have your house working too while you live in it (only with my system).

Turning your Principal Place of Residence (your home) into a working asset will make you better off.

There are lots of negatives associated with conventional loans that banks or their compatriots never tell you about. One of the big one's is the mortgage document! Very few of us ever go through the process of having the clauses explained by a lawyer. A costly process and who wants to be depressed when you have already saved for the deposit and conveyancing. As far as I know there are no clauses protecting the borrower. A bit silly to expect otherwise I suppose given that the document is prepared for the **lender by his solicitor or Legal Department.** Naturally it doesn't come into play if everything goes smoothly. However, sometimes life can serve up a curve ball that is difficult to deal with. We have already discussed the "all monies" clause which can wreak havoc but there are other nasties which I will do my best to identify.

The major one's are as follows:

- Remember the mortgage is for the lenders protection not yours. The "on demand" clause is straight forward i.e. if you get in trouble, we (the lender) don't want to know about it, therefore you can repay the loan immediately. Obviously with home ownership being the great Australian dream, a more caring approach is now required. The modern-day approach adopted by all lending institutions is better but doesn't go far enough. After-all, the bank must maintain profitability. Despite this fact, this is an all-powerful

clause - I would not trust a **lender** not to use it in an extreme case.
- Losing your job at the wrong time especially one that is essential for servicing a home loan is bad news at any-time. This can obviously be even more devastating if a sole breadwinner in a family situation is involved. As far as I know clauses covering lenders **"hardship"** have never been exceeded i.e. lenders and banks meet the minimum requirements and no more. From my knowledge their hardship policy is certainly nothing to write home about - 3 months paying interest only then catch-up what you are behind. In lots of circumstances this is totally inadequate. There is undoubtedly some circumstance where 'hardship' provisions greater than the above are allowed. However why not avoid 'hardship' altogether with my system.
- Clauses in the mortgage covering linking of debts and cross collateralising of the different properties which secure those debts (assuming there is more than one debt). The latter activity is a favoured ploy by all home lenders - with this they have all bases covered and the borrower has little or no say in the outcome. In my view this is **totally wrong and counter-productive to the borrower (and his family) coming back from financial strife.**

- The "all monies" clause has already been discussed but it's devastating ramifications cannot be over emphasised. I have personal experience in this area. I can assure you that some clown in a sell-up department is going to act according to what he believes is in the lenders best interests. The borrower's wishes will be given scant consideration. In a past life I was a borrower and the lender (a major bank) told me a whole lot of lies and did what they liked to my ultimate detriment. I am hopeful that one day the so-called Big 4 will be held accountable for their dirty tricks. The only thing that they serve is the mighty dollar - of course that is a bit harsh, but I must remind you that they are all public companies listed on the stock exchange. The real owners are shareholders who have different priorities. Please be very mindful of what I said earlier - if there is any subsequent loan it is automatically linked to the original (that could be the family home loan) and the **whole debt is secured by the first mortgage document signed**. In the absence of signing any mortgage for the second borrowing the whole debt is still secured. You can thank the "all monies" clause in the original document for that.

- There are plenty of other clauses all looking after the lender which I won't bother going into. As far as I know there are not too many looking after the borrower. (After all the mortgage document is prepared for the Lender's protection).

Anybody can make a mistake! We are all fallible and without prior knowledge about how an investment purchase can go bad, it would be hard to know that using the same lender is also a mistake. You have to sign the same mortgage over the family home but with my system the bank manager and school (where your kids go if you have any) will never know you have lost your job or for that matter when you have changed employment. It is none of their business anyway. My system H/L gets rid of any mortgage stress on both occasions. Naturally when you lose a job without warning there is a period of introspection when you might blame yourself. This is a natural reaction! The last thing a home-buyer needs is all the other "baggage" and the whole neighbourhood knowing.

My system enables you to remove mortgage stress from the equation and simply get on with your life. Losing a job is hard enough and shouldn't create terrible thoughts like "here I go I could lose everything".

Such thoughts would be justified with a conventional mortgage as advance loan payments is the only real insurance against loss. If you have a needy family or an extravagant wife or both or just can't get ahead with the loan (as many will attest to) the only option left in a crisis is family. This is sometimes just a very awkward silence.

My financial system avoids all this financial angst and turmoil.

Putting negative equity aside property values go up and down all the time especially in a large land mass like Australia. We have not experienced real inflation for a long time but could simply inherit it from the USA. We have in the past! It will doubtless appear whether we like it or not. When it does property values are impacted negatively especially house prices - in my opinion this would at least end the upward spiral in Sydney property prices. What has happened in the past is a good indication of what we can expect in the future. This is not a rosy outlook, but it is how I am thinking. The reality is that property values go up and down all the time for lots of economic reasons.

GDP for the Australian economy goes up and down with the cost of raw materials on World markets.

Shares go up and down and so does everything else so don't think the family home is immune - its value will fluctuate like everything else. Only over time do houses go up in value - it is a long-term thing. In the short term wide fluctuations in value can occur. One thing in the H/L market that is a good thing for homebuyers is that a good valuation on the day will ensure that just about any refinance will be approved and proceed. The other good thing for the buyer is that if he buys at the seller's asking price this is universally accepted as its market value unless something is amiss with the property. Buy your investment property whenever you like - with my system you will have the cash and remember "cash is king" at any-time. When you have cash, the purchase is always cheaper. A seller naturally feels better with a confident cash buyer and a lower price is invariably negotiated.

The fact is that when you decide to shift your loan to a new lender a fresh valuation is ordered to ensure no loss of equity. The new lender will only approve the move if there is sufficient equity. There are many other factors but the impediment of a "break cost" would stifle any transfer to a different Conventional loan. The "break cost" is paid by the borrower. Payment of such a cost would only be justified if you were transferring to one of my H/L systems.

Break costs are a penalty that borrowers pay if the whole or part of their loan is fixed, and they want to shift their loan. Banks and non-bank lenders are fully aware of this situation and stand ready to fully exploit this for their own benefit i.e. they know that if the loan is fixed or a portion of it is fixed then it likely that they will retain the facility. Borrowers as a group are very unlikely to shift knowing that the break cost is theirs to pay. Borrowers fix interest rates on their loan for entirely different reasons i.e. if rates are historically low as they are now, or they think rates are going up soon. I reiterate that shifting to another lender with a conventional loan is a waste of time. Shifting to my home loan system would be justified at any figure - the reward would be life changing. You can still fix most of your loan after refinancing with me.

Conventional loans have always had too many drawbacks for me. Don't have any doubts about its inflexibility - it's quite intentional. A lenders investment loan is the same as the loan for the family home. The only difference is that the investment loan is usually interest only for your tax claim.

The banks including the Big 4 plus all the non-bank lenders want a simple transaction. A Conventional loan is just that - the borrower gets the house and the lender gets a long-term repayable loan (and a return on the principal loan and prime first mortgage security). The problem is it creates the "them" and "us" syndrome. My home loan system does away with that mentality i.e. the borrower takes control and makes all the decisions (with some initial assistance from me until they know what's going on and that's not long) and the bank and or bank manager is removed permanently.

I haven't processed a Conventional loan for at least 20 years. The reason is simple! When applicants see my product, they reject the Conventional home loan because of its inferiority. Please understand I am not decrying a conventional loan just for fun - it is only designed to get the house. If it had a few other benefits that look after the borrower it wouldn't be so bad. Sadly it doesn't look after the borrower half as well as it should. In any event it is no match for my product in this or any other area. My product settles the transaction in the same way and then because it is a genuine wealth creation system has a life-time of benefits going forward. You will have access to cash without ever having to ask the bank manager (his permission is no longer required or appropriate).

A conventional loan will never give you financial freedom.

Australian banks and especially the Big 4 make huge profits. The so-called Big 4 make billions not millions and they don't do it by going easy on borrowers. Be smart and realise that you don't have to re-invent the wheel to get ahead. I have been in finance all my life and have a "tried and true" product that does everything I say it does (refer the many benefits listed in the next chapter). I wouldn't have written two books sending one all over Australia if my home loan system didn't work. I have also established these systems in the market place for more than 25 years. My refinance (or new house) loan is a home loan with a different set-up. It is not shrouded in mystery (it's a home loan).

The Royal Commission into financial institutions especially the Big 4 Banks has certainly shone the torch on their activities. Attracting business is important to all of us but chasing profits at the expense of people/customers is the aspect that I think is most damming. There is no doubt in my mind that the banks have been guilty of this however, it is a capitalist society and every entity and employer of people has to remain profitable. At the same time, I think that banks generally and the

Big 4 in particular can afford to scale it back a bit. After-all, looking after the individual, not just saying you do is important. It's like the old saying "have a nice day" – I'm sure that half the people that say it mean the opposite. Look at the farmers! It's really good that the whole community is now listening and starting to help. The farmers are the producers and we can no longer stick our heads in the sand. There is a crippling drought and we all have to take some responsibility. The heavy handed approach of certain banks is no longer acceptable. Many events have been high-lighted in the news. It would be good if the banks did something positive.

The latest excuse for loan default by one of the Big 4 Banks is that the loan process might not be rigorous enough in relation to living expenses. I am totally mystified by this statement and will go on record saying that it would be impossible to identify under- statement of living expenses as a reason for default. The actual reason for default could be due to any number of factors including irresponsible lending which is common and a topic that is discussed in detail in this book. Banks are a bit like doctors in that they bury their mistakes. A bank saying that understatement of living expenses could be the reason for defaults doesn't make it a fact. Many more questions have to be asked. What was the original loan amount? When was it approved? When did the default occur? What were the circumstances? Was the problem the family home loan? Did the borrower own investment properties? Were they fully let? Were there any vacancies? Did financial difficulty first appear with the investment loan? Default is a complex issue and is never due to just one thing. Questions always need to be asked in an effort to identify the real cause of default. In this instance under estimating living expenses hasn't been justified and looks like a load of codswallop.

Obviously, there would be instances where something is missed in the loan process – this would rarely or never be the reason for a borrower falling over. A borrower may inadvertently understate something or his actions might be deliberate, after-all he is trying to get a loan approval. Nevertheless, it would undoubtedly be something small and never the reason for default.

Assuming basic eligibility, a deposit in hand plus solicitor's conveyancing costs potential borrowers have a lot at stake. Understatement of living expenses may occur on the odd occasion – the borrower in question may turn out to be one of the best at repaying the loan. As it is I believe the link between under stated living expenses and loan default is not proven. **The Big Banks statement is discounted entirely and there is certainly no case for making the loan process more invasive than it already is.**

Approval of a loan is vital to any application, home loan or otherwise. There is little doubt that loans could be made harder to get. In many instances repayment of a loan has nothing to do with what is written down. Some people simply rise to the occasion – all you might see at the initial interview is a steely resolve that turns into a great loan performance. Nothing on paper! Only one bank has used understatement of living expenses as a reason for default. I think the Major Bank in question should go it alone and make its own H/L process harder. They will then lose custom on their own. A good thing given that they are one of those organizations proud of making billions. If something does happen hopefully customers will go to some of the smaller players in the finance industry and benefit from them.

All in all, I think it is a devious ploy and also think there is absolutely no case for making the loan process more arduous than it already is. I am being a bit repetitive on this issue as I feel strongly that there is no case for change.

It is a pity that borrowers don't have a uniform voice. I am affronted by the whole episode – a dummy spit by one of our Major Banks. Nothing said excuses poor lending and that is certainly rife in the ………….. industry. I think that one of the reasons that they have a bad name is that they don't really care about people or not enough (perhaps its profits). I have a dislike for banks and believe the old saying "banks are good at taking the umbrella away when it starts to rain" i.e. fair weather friends.

I have had no sell ups with my system H/L's in a long career in finance. Undoubtedly, there have been periods where standards of assessment have been less than what they are today. Nevertheless, none of my borrowers have fallen through the cracks and I am definitely not bleating about under stated living expenses.

I have been in finance 50+ years! In my view a financial institutions job is to provide credit. If it does its job properly there will be few arrears. In the current situation we have a major bank (making billions) crying poor. **Perhaps it is a little bank after-all.**

As with any Conventional loan you will need a clear credit rating to get one of my set-ups. The same people that approve Conventional loans approve my facility- after-all, my facility is a H/L but a clever variation with a different set-up. If you are concerned about defaults and want them removed, give me a call. There are organisations that deal directly with the governing body- a good solicitor can also get a clear credit rating for a client.

The thing to remember is that even minor credit blemishes can prevent further loans from going ahead. It is not clear cut, but some approvals have occurred on a case by case basis when defaults are minor.

If you have any defaults, then you can be assured they will surface (the credit reference system is watertight).

The following chapter is the most important in this short book. It sets out my Privacy Act requirements plus a list of the many benefits that the users of my home loan system have enjoyed over the last 25 years. The list is not exhaustive, and somebody out there will no-doubt think of something else that can be achieved. A Conventional loan has no bells and whistles and is only designed for one thing and one thing only (to get the house).

The real problem in this modern era is that it is totally inadequate in too many other areas. My H/L system also gets the house but is a wealth creating instrument thereafter and looks after the borrower in a lot of other fundamental areas i.e. far more versatility.

I hope you really enjoy the next chapter- it has been written with a view to getting the borrower a far better deal.

Chapter Two

MY UNIQUE HOME LOAN PRODUCT - A WEALTH CREATING HOME LOAN

From what you have already read it is not hard to fathom that I am a financial person. I have followed my father. He was a very gifted financial person who passed on certain attributes to me.

As a direct result of my father's influence and direction, I have spent fifty years in the finance industry. I have a depth of experience acquired over a long period and am serious about passing what I know on. I am sure this is what has led me to the loan system and writing this book. I previously had a website which set out the benefits of the system but the name Low Doc Mortgages.com.au was not mine and it was subsequently closed. I do own the Infinity Mortgage dot com. and that will probably be my next project. The benefits of this system were listed under a section headed 'The Infinity Mortgage' which is an appropriate name for this concept.

Irrespective of my time in finance I know I have something vital that must be passed on. I would first like to emphasise the following:

(1) I have been involved in most facets of finance, i.e. from hire purchase, to leasing to personal loans (secured and unsecured) plus Home Lending. I was also heavily involved in commercial lending and in it for a lot longer than home lending. In my early days in Townsville I handled the finance on a shopping centre in Aitkenvale. I couldn't do it any more as you need separate accreditations with every commercial lender you use. I shopped the deal to Westpac, NAB and some other bank but in the end got a better deal from Suncorp the client's existing banker and he stayed with them.

(2) I was the Senior Loans Officer at Chancery House branch in Bourke Street, Melbourne and pencilled for The Manager for Victoria CBA (commercial loans).

(3) I had a portfolio of loans in a Merchant bank and had further experience in writing commercial loans with them.

(4) I rose to a Senior Consultant with Aussie Home Loans and wrote many loans for that organisation.

(5) I hold a current credit licence number 387895 with ASIC. Actually that is in my company's name and I am the sole director. I also hold a certificate (iv) in lending and was offered an honorary diploma in finance by Intellitrain (a recognised educator). I was with Home Loan Connexion and their aggregator Australian Finance Group for say 25 years. I was also with Vow Financial but am now referring loans to a different organization. I am a member of the Credit Ombudsman Service of Australia re dispute resolutions in finance and the FBAA (Finance Brokers Association of Australia). You must be a member of the FBAA or the MFAA (Mortgage & Finance Association of Australia) to be a finance broker in this country.

My system provides a freedom that simply doesn't exist with a conventional home loan. A conventional loan is a very structured way of buying your own house generally through a bank, building society, cooperative, mortgage manager or other home lender. The loan is generally a principal and interest arrangement over thirty years or shorter if you throw a lot of cash at it. If you are fortunate enough to purchase an investment property using equity from another property or your family home, then the lender will automatically cross collateralise both mortgages. That means that both properties are tied up. Obviously you would want to avoid this. Even if you own multiple properties, linking of them simply does not happen with my system. The system also does not disturb any existing investment you may have other than something quite outside the norm and it's probably okay even then.

The system applies to both self-employed individuals (Corporate, Trust or otherwise), and PAYG income earners alike and can be used by all income earners into retirement when normal income ceases. Banks and other lenders normally look for loan repayment when your income or self-employed income ceases, i.e. retirement. Why not continue with property investment after you retire when you can have some real fun, make lots of money and share it around with your family (as most of us are inclined to do). This system has no down side and only needs to be set up on your principal place of residence which can be upgraded at any time. If the only property you have is an investment one then you can set up my loan system on it. It still works!

The system has universal appeal but as a home loan originator product it cannot be secured by rural or farm properties or commercially-zoned property.

There are no tax advantages on a loan over your principal place of residence but there is the usual tax relief on all the investment properties you acquire. It is your own home and the facility that you set up on it that leads to the purchase of all the investment properties. My system loan on your house also gives you access to cash and many other things. You don't have to buy a lot of investment houses. That is entirely your choice! Just pay your home loan off in your time frame not the lenders (and a lot quicker if you wish). You can also use cash in the system to buy all of your cars, expensive cars if that is what you want—or other items and consumer durables. I had a BMW M3 as well as $15M in real estate which I got applying the system. I haven't got it now but you can bet I will be starting up again shortly.

The uses and benefits of the system are many. You can use some of your retirement funds to double or triple your money. Before outlining in depth the substantial benefits that accrue to users of this system I will go through privacy requirements generally. There are two lots. You will automatically sign a privacy form in the lenders application. This is the same with all loans, (conventional or otherwise) in this country. So you sign a conventional privacy form and my privacy form if you want a loan system. My privacy form for a system loan is set out below:

> Addressed to me
> Re: Loan System—Privacy Act
> I/we refer to our recent discussion regarding a possible loan facility and hereby freely sign this privacy declaration prior to being shown the system. I/we fully understand that details of the system are not to be communicated in any way to any other person, financial person or institution and or finance broker under any circumstances.
>
> This privacy form simply enables me to pass on details of my loan system—our subsequent acceptance or rejection of it is up to us.
> I/we acknowledge and agree that particulars of the loan system are provided for our consideration **only** and no particulars or diagrams are to be discussed or given to any other party.

This brief privacy form is signed generally by two people (husband and wife)—a small alteration is made by me when a corporate or self-employed entity is involved. A partnership is dealt with in a similar way to individuals as long as no companies are involved.

Please understand that this system is tried and true. I was forced to sell my AFG trail book for cash but every second loan on that list involved a systems loan. There were about six pages of loans with fifty entries to a page which means that a lot of people had system loans with me.

I will now set out the benefits of my system loan in detail. They are many, and once again I emphasise that a conventional loan has no discernible benefits apart from helping you with the original purchase. I say this with a lot of confidence having been in finance for as long as I have and writing both types of loans. The main benefits are:

- Removes mortgage stress associated with a normal home loan.

Mortgage stress relates to loan repayments. In this case we are talking about home loans but the term can apply to any loan repayable to a lender. Because the normal home loan is advanced at the outset repayment is made up of two components i.e. principal and interest. Both are usually paid monthly to meet the lenders minimum requirements. At the outset the loan repayment is almost all interest. As the loan reduces it reverses and the loan principal falls faster and there is a smaller interest component. Mortgage stress is best described as the effect loan repayments can have on the borrower. It would be quite natural to think that the bigger the loan the greater the stress but income is an important factor (and you can only borrow what you can repay i.e. based on the lenders guidelines). Despite servicing being based on income larger loans can be a headache for borrowers anyway. There are many factors that intrude. Obviously, it is important that borrowers structure their home loan debt in the most comfortable way (so repayments are relatively easy). A lot of people don't attend to this issue properly. At the same time this is a two edged sword – a loan can be all variable interest rate (I/R), or all fixed (I/R) or a mixture of both. A variable rate loan can be repaid the quickest however it is subject to I/R swings as determined by our Central Bank (The Reserve Bank of Australia – it sits monthly and rules on I/R's each month). The Reserve Bank has traditionally looked at a whole range of issues including inflation. This latter aspect has been a major concern in the past but it isn't at present – I/R's have in fact been steady for a record number of months (in the absence of inflation). This time other economic factors have kept house prices down. Wages growth is one factor but this has been virtually non-existent in recent years. Whilst minimal wages growth is a real negative for a lot of people at least it has helped with inflation. When inflation is under control property values are more stable and I/R's are generally lower. The lender is OK in all situations as he simply passes on any increase in interest rate to the borrower. After-all, it is his responsibility (along with loan repayments).

Mortgage stress is closely related to loan structure so it is important for the borrower to get it right especially when the amount borrowed is substantial. For instance if we have a borrower that believes he can clear $200K quickly he might establish an $800K loan with $200K on a variable I/R and the balance of $600K on a lower fixed rate. He can then proceed with a level of confidence should interest rates go against him i.e. go up. Interest rates are very low at present so all they can really do is go up – in the past I/R's have been higher and rate changes much more difficult to pick (up or down).

I believe that the biggest risk for all borrowers (mortgage stress) is when interest rates change. Upward movements can be very hard to predict and I/R's can do the opposite to what is expected. I bumped into an old client years ago that fixed the rate on a large portion of his H/L. He locked in a rate of 8.5% for 3 years! Rates were expected to go up! Interest rates did the opposite and went down. Just about everybody was paying 6% while he was paying the higher rate. I met this guy by chance in the Townsville Mall one-day and he blamed me. I certainly didn't tell him to fix his loan but needless to say never saw him again.

If you live in the mortgage belt of Sydney, Melbourne and to a lesser extent Brisbane where prices of homes tend to be a lot higher a .5% increase can result in an additional $300 per month on the mortgage repayment. A lot to find in a hurry! Interest rates are reviewed by The RBA every month (and everybody wants to avoid arrears and any lender backlash). Of course mortgages in those Cities tend to be bigger than those in other places. That's right big property values equate with big mortgages.

Of course mortgage stress can increase exponentially if the key income of the borrower(s) is lost or reduced.

My H/L system does away with mortgage stress. The borrower(s) may have 6 to 12 months or longer to replace an income. The safety margin is determined by the borrower(s) at the outset.

Mortgage stress is a **huge** issue for borrowers with what's currently in the market.

It is my view that borrowers no longer have the resilience to meet higher rates – years ago (in the 80's) H/L interest rates exceeded 15%p.a.

People with a normal mortgage could lose their houses (and this could happen on a large scale). Again, this is really only one of the borrower's worries although the lender or his insurer will carry any resulting bad debt.

You will avoid this situation and mortgage stress with one of my H/L systems.

- This loan system can refinance any existing loan over residential property.

To clarify this matter further my system can refinance any existing H/L (secured by first mortgage) after six months has elapsed – the **new lender** requires loan statements for the same period to confirm good conduct (and to ensure all repayments have been made on time), a fresh valuation plus all the other paraphernalia required to get approval. To purchase your first family home or purchase any other residential property after that (to live in or otherwise) the process is just like any other H/L application. In fact, unless the property is a real lemon, the valuer will adopt purchase price as valuation. It is easier than a refinance loan from this point of view. **My system H/L is subject to the same process.**

- Only one set up on your own home or principal place of residence (purchase of investment properties are dealt with later).

My wealth creation system (a home loan) is the only one of its type allowing you to make money, make lifestyle improvements and change your life and that of your family forever and acquire investment properties etc. **all from my H/L and your FAMILY HOME while you live in it.**

Think of your family and yourself, the promise of a better life is as close as refinancing your existing home loan or purchasing a family home using my home loan system.

- Clears your existing debt and gives you access to other funds (in cash).

This very important benefit relates to your access to other funds, your own salaries (borrowers) **all in cash.** You and you alone will be able to pay cash and take the family on a world trip, pay a cash deposit on an investment property, finance the purchase of a new car or buy a new lounge suite etc. The benefit and access to ready cash cannot be over-emphasised.

Everybody knows that CASH or money makes the world go round – access to more of it will change your life for the better.

- Maximise your interest rate concession.

This concession will be self-evident when you draw down on your new home loan (my system). **Any concession in interest rate is determined by the lender and by the size of the loan.**

- Turn your principal place of residence into a wealth creation instrument.

This is a specific reference to the borrowers family home i.e. your **Principal Place of Residence.** The principal place of residence is the **best** place to have one of my H/L systems.

If you don't have a family home but do own an investment property then you can still put one of my home loan systems on that property. You will still enjoy the same benefits!

- Lodge/withdraw amounts at any time so that you pay less interest on your home loan. A boon for self-employed individuals who can lodge and withdraw funds from their business at any time to save on **personal interest costs** (where no taxation benefits exist).

Only business owners that have a family or investment home can access this colossal benefit.

At the same time there are many people in this situation in Australia i.e. people that own their own home and later operate a successful business or vice versa, those that have first had the business and then want to purchase a family home.

This involves accessing a portion of your business turnover (cash in the business that is not being used) to reduce the personal interest on your home loan. It is entirely legal for the owner of the business as he makes all the decisions and simple if he is the **borrower and has my system**.

- Only pay on the net amount owing.

This benefit is self-evident and appears shortly after my system is put in place.

- Create a surplus pool of funds for investment or any purpose that you deem worthwhile. You only do this with the advantage of specialised knowledge—the loan system is not for gambling.

This particular benefit is closely aligned with comments made on a previous benefit (bullet point). Clearly you can buy anything with cash but smart people only buy what they want and don't take unnecessary risks.

- Being cashed up you are in a position to invest at the right price at the right time and at any time.

Having access to cash is **KING** – the price is always lower if you have cash.

- Because you have access to cash—buy cheap when everybody else is selling their investments.

Whilst this might seem the same as the previous bullet point – it is just another aspect to having cash. When you have cash you will always get the best deal. What this clause is really getting at is that the availability of cash means **you are buying when everybody is selling and vice versa you are selling when everybody else is buying** (and paying more to you because there are plenty of buyers and you are not desperate for cash). Having cash is good at any time!

- Purchase investment properties when they are at rock bottom price and in a way that is not possible with a conventional loan (no cross collateralising of properties). You make all the decisions but without a bank manager looking over your shoulder. Please note that people with a conventional loan rarely buy an investment property. Their setup doesn't allow them to and they are too busy trying to pay off their home loan quickly.

Again, purchase of an investment property at a "rock bottom" price is achieved every-time with a cash deposit (the vendor will love you). The other part of the equation is also solved with my system i.e. the purchase is finalised and **isolated from all other property transactions (no cross collateralising of securities).**

Probably the most important issue is that with my system **you the borrower(s) make all the decisions.** You decide when to buy and there will be nobody around to trip you up (including the friendly bank manager). You will have cash for the deposit and be making all the decisions re purchase of investment properties and anything else that has your focus.

- Sell investment properties in your timeframe with maximum taxation benefits/deductions and a minimum outlay for capital gains tax (if applicable). Afterwards you simply put surplus funds to maximum benefit in any account of your choice.

The whole purpose of purchasing an investment property is to make a profit. If there is a little man in your head saying not to buy a **particular property** then don't buy it. Everything must feel right especially the bit about making a profit. I have seen the worst thing happen. A fellow I used to know purchased an investment property using equity from his family home to complete settlement. I believe that the "all monies" clause in the first mortgage (over the family home) is the reason he lost the lot. Firstly, the property he purchased declined $50/60,000 in value and the equity that he had in the family home evaporated over-night. If this hadn't happened he could perhaps have offset the loss against the family home and its mortgage however, it was very sad and everything went South. Actually, I think he got a bit of help from somebody but had to start again anyway (renting).

Remember, it is essential to make a **profit. At the same** time any-body can make a mistake with a property purchase and that is why **each** one must be **isolated** from every other investment purchase. If you have numerous investment properties you can always sell one to clear a loss on the other. If you have one of my H/L systems on the family home and your first investment purchase is a mistake but it is isolated **(as it would be with my system)** access to cash may be enough to get you out of trouble. If you are lucky parents on both sides might be able to chip in and help you keep the family home. Mistakes are part of life and will make you more knowledgeable and on the ball next time.

When selling an investment property make sure your timing is right i.e. don't finish with the tenant at the wrong time. If the selling period looks like being poor when the rental is due to expire renew for another two years with the current tenant or get a new tenant. Depending on where the property location is, selling at the wrong time might simply crystalize a bad result.

- Minimum repayments that should be less than what you are currently paying on your home loan.

This is a self-evident and you will become aware of it when my H/L system is established.

- Implement an accelerated repayment program at any time and repay your loan in your timeframe (not the lenders/banks).

You can start repaying your loan quickly and the lender won't even be aware of it. Repaying H/L debt is easy and I will show you how to accelerate repayments. You will be able to leverage funds from other sources including your own income and really get things moving – you would have to win Tattslotto with a traditional loan facility.

- Repay home loan debt quickly (5 years) or at whatever speed that suits you.

Clearance of H/L debt in record time depends on many factors. All I will say is I have seen a blistering repayment performance on more than one occasion. A good example of debt clearance in less than 2 years is quoted in this book. Certainly a loan term of say 5/10 years is easily achieved.

- Purchase other properties for investment with full taxation benefits. The original credit provider may not be used as you will have the required equity in cash. You will get away from the mentality of using your own bank to acquire property. This financial structure will allow you to get the best possible deal available fom any number of different lenders.

The underlying benefit in this bullet point is a **real benefit that relates to decision making.** You will be making all the decisions and will have a better understanding and knowledge especially with respect to property transactions. All human beings are better with the next transaction and they benefit from repetition i.e. practice in sport makes us better. The friendly bank manager is great! However there is a difficulty – he wants to help but he also answers to the heirachy of the bank. He is therefore conflicted in many situations! **Your decisions are therefore better for you.** I can assure you that you don't need anybody telling you what to do. The bank manager's property savvy is soon learnt and you will be immensely better off without his advice. Making your own decisions is a big part of my system. Run your own show you will be far better off as a result.

It is my job as a finance professional to provide accurate property advice to investors and home buyers so that my home loan system operates successfully for them. This is the job of every mortgage broker.

- Keep this loan system for 5, 10, 30 years or a lifetime and into retirement.

Again this is self-evident after using my H/L system.

- Remember this loan structure has a life time of usefulness—most other home loans are not useful, you simply pay them off over a life time.

My system H/L is distinctly different from the H/L you have now. Anything that is in market at the present time is just a normal housing loan – you get the house **and the loan commitment**. No matter how you source the loan I can assure you it is the 30 year deal (they all are). If you use all your resources you can take 4 years off the loan by making fortnightly repayments.

My way is incomparably better.

- Lose your job or jobs and don't lose your house (disaster with a conventional loan).

This bullet point and removal of mortgage stress from H/L borrowings is one of the cornerstones of my H/L system.

Mortgage stress and job loss are dealt with in this book in great detail. There are so many other great benefits however – access to cash, repay H/L debt in record time, improve and change your lifestyle forever, make lots of money in retirement and taking control of your own destiny etc.

Whilst I have discussed 20 odd benefits of my wealth creating home loan there are further uses that can be identified – sometimes a combination of more than one benefit will make it work for you. If you are thinking of doing up the family home prior to sale and have a conventional home loan. Then the local bank manager will undoubtedly be your first port of call especially if you haven't got the cash to do the renovation yourself.

He will have to share your views and will only give you the money if you have usable equity in your family home. In the absence of equity he will not be able to assist. Of course, an un-secured personal loan could be considered at a higher rate of interest but that will land you with another loan commitment that may not be affordable. If the bank manager shares your view that expenditures will add value to the property he might suggest proceeding as follows: appoint a builder with a formal fixed price contract – the bank may then say it will consider approval subject to a satisfactory "on completion" valuation. If revaluation provides the additional equity the bank will assist. **An expensive exercise any way you look at it, with a lot of "ifs" and no guarantee of approval – by the way all the costs are yours not the banks.**

Even if you get a conventional approval the bank manager will be making all sorts of enquiries before it is finalised. Are you up-grading the family home for a larger one? Are you staying in the area? Are you moving away? Are you changing employment? Is there a promotion? My H/L system avoids all this aggravation.

You will have access to cash and will know exactly when to go ahead with renovations. In addition, any up-grade will be your decision. Asking somebody else like the bank manager will be a thing of the past.

I had a good friend in the Army that did exactly what I have said. He is now a Major in Canberra. He had my system, up-graded his house with cash and later sold. All without a bank manager! Actually he had a nice place in Townsville prior to his Canberra transfer. He was divorced with custody of two kids most of the time. His house was in a very quiet area with a pool, separate bedrooms for the kids and a council maintained park at the rear (like an extended backyard).

I actually thought the place looked pretty shabby until Mic made the decision to up-grade and move on. **His decision,** with a surprisingly small amount of cash transformed the house (and what a transformation). The place sold quickly and he got thousands more than expected. He up-graded to a big 2 storey place in Kirwan! He had a great attitude! and also had an investment unit close to Stockland Plaza (Townsville's most prestigious Shopping Centre).

With my system in place he used cash to up-grade, sold and purchased a much bigger family home. All his cash and decisions were without a bank manager. Incidentally I paid for his valuation report on the new place. Work on the old place was all undertaken at Mic's direction - subcontracting everything. There were no contracts or anything else. He probably saved $10K by doing all the subcontracting himself.

The second thing is also a use of my system i.e. when you are disposing of an investment property. Every property can be made to look better prior to sale. Even a lick of paint! In most cases you can put more in and make the place look a lot better. Often the sale price will be surprising – perhaps a little extra carpentry will fetch another $20K. If you are not pressed for time you should always try to get a little more. **Remember the only reason for purchasing an investment house in the first place is to make a profit.**

Turning over the family vehicle is a big deal in most households. The whole cost thing is a lot easier with a normal family vehicle costing $35 to $40K. Later in life, I bought a BMW M3 involving a big cash outlay. Everything is so much easier when the numbers are smaller. With my system you can use cash and drive new vehicles, turning them over every ¾ years for the latest model. This is a life style decision and one that I have **never seen except with my system.** The bank manager would be horrified as he can't do it himself. Don't worry he won't know!

After you have paid off the family home, acquired a few investment houses and accumulated a bit of cash the pressure really falls away. You can enjoy everything a lot more! If you haven't quite paid off the family home you can tidy that up with a bit of Super and give your kids a hand out to make life a bit easier for them. Remember, you can continue to make money with my home loan system in retirement and also have a much better time.

In retirement you have less to worry about and no job! All of this is out of the question with an ordinary loan. Usually, the bank or its manager expects all loans to be repaid when there is no income i.e. in retirement.

One of the really terrific things about my system is that the bank or its manager will also never know your age.

We should talk about multiplying your Superannuation payout after retirement. Again, you can earn far more than any Superannuation Fund will by taking a cash payout or part thereof at retirement. You will then become an **expert** in another field (if you are not already) and earn much more money. You may think I am joking but I am not, you really will be an **expert.** The Oxford Dictionary definition of an expert is a person having great knowledge or skill in a particular field. You will certainly reach that status.

A wealthy friend of mine had his accounts at ANZ. I am pretty sure that he banked with them for many years with numerous undertakings including a successful bakery. He was a fully qualified accountant and knew what he was doing. Anyway the manager took it on himself to close an account without asking his customer. Roger was incensed and now banks with CBA. **You can really do without an interfering bank manager.**

There are many more uses to be had with my system via a combination of benefits (refer the 20 bullet points already discussed).

Please understand that I am not knocking banks/lenders that help you get a family home to live in. You can get the same family home with one of my system loans and own it outright a lot quicker. This system ensures you keep it even if you lose your job (as above)—afterwards your house then works for you (for a life-time).

The aspects of job-loss have already been covered so the next few comments are a bit repetitive. This is to emphasise the crisis it can cause. If you are unfortunate and lose your job and can't immediately replace it, you are in a world of hurt with a conventional loan. The situation is worse if you are the sole breadwinner and have no ability to meet even interest (the basic requirement of hardship with any lender-bank). You can then be looking at a sell up. As well, please don't confuse mortgage insurance—it only covers the lender or bank in the event of them sustaining a loss. When you are sold up this doesn't cover you.

You lose your house and any deposit you may have put in, (if there is any negative equity when all this goes down, then it would be included in the overall loss and covered by mortgage insurance)—as long as you had it in the first place. That aspect would not be of concern, but being out on the street with nothing is. In this country if the mortgage insurer is still short he can bankrupt you. I know what it's like to owe money and it's certainly a humbling experience.

The system will be of untold benefit to you financially if you own and operate a business of your own. In all cases that I know of, (and I was in commercial lending for years), you can put almost all your turnover through your home loan to save on interest costs—again, impossible with a conventional loan. You don't take funds or cash out of your business account if there is no benefit. The pay-off for this is huge with a system loan on your house. It is only smart and good business practice to hold a small amount in your business account with which to pay creditors.

Do you need an overdraft for your business which is cheap and never reviewed by the lender? This topic will need to be discussed with you in detail when we catch up. I will mention that there is one more thing on this matter which is important. There is absolutely no benefit in carrying large credit balances in a business account (the bank will love you as they lend money against depositor's balances—however, forget the bank, it makes enough profit without you).

If you are paying off your home and fancy your carpentry skills, you can use them to create more equity in your home and then convert that increased equity into cash. The latter is a great idea with the loan system, but almost impossible with a conventional loan.

I would like to make a few observations and say that I have been really straight with any reader of this book. I have provided you a snap shot of my life willingly and can simply say that finance is all I know, (apart from golf). The system itself is an honest one. I have spent a lifetime in this industry and have always been attempting to help people get ahead with their finances, (not hinder them).

Before licencing with ASIC there were a lot of cowboys in the industry more concerned with their own bottom line than yours. In some cases, this descended into outright dishonesty. I would only bore you with the multitude of dubious practices that went on—there were many. I was always looking out for the eligible client and trying to get the best outcome for him. Quite frankly I would never have lasted as long in finance if I didn't have a legitimate interest in helping people.

This system is about helping you **big-time** and it is tried and true as I have already mentioned. I have performed these loan systems exclusively over the last twenty years, and I could just as easily have set up a conventional loan. That's what finance brokers do!

All the same, conventional loans are very limited in what they can achieve, and nobody selects one of them once they are privy to one of my loan systems. I get questions like "Can I really buy that car with cash?" or" how much cash I should keep in reserve?" or "can I put a cash deposit on that investment property?" You really can do a multitude of things with a system loan and nothing with a conventional loan. You control everything not the lender.

A few years ago, the major banks sold up a whole lot of first home buyers on the Manly Peninsula in Sydney. Although there was limited press about it, and of course it is natural for them to try and avoid as much negative press as possible, people then tend to go elsewhere for their home loans (credit unions, etc.). Manly Peninsula is a very sought-after part of Sydney and houses are expensive. Borrowers would lose serious money, i.e. $35K on a 5% deposit or $70K on a 10% deposit plus legal expenses (apart from any negative equity). Borrowers are the only real losers when there is a sell up. From memory I think there were about 700 sell ups on the Manly Peninsula. I venture to say that none of those people would have been sold up had they been on my home loan system.

Everyone needs a home loan to get a house. The only exception to this is the rich and famous or anyone lucky enough to win Tatts-lotto. Traditionally, people have gone to the banks including the Big 4 and a multitude of non-bank lenders for a Conventional loan. This has been the only product at their disposal for the past 50/60 years. **I want you to break with tradition and fully investigate my product** – it is superior in every way and reduces the clear advantage that lenders currently have over borrowers. This advantage is **unfair and should be**

changed simply on the basis of results. The results of the H/L borrower with my set up are incomparably better from every aspect. A borrower obtains financial security and the lender is involved in no discernible sell ups - a better result for everyone. At present a traditional home loan is used to acquire an asset which can quickly turn into a liability.

I am not a particularly religious person. Anything to do with religion is man-made and that speaks for itself. This can be good or bad—some of the worst human beings in the World are Bible basher's (hypocrites). I am sure that most of them would go to church. In the so-called Dark Ages churches used to burn people at the stake. These days there are a lot of paedophiles in churches—most people these days think churches are respectable—they probably are but you still have to come to that conclusion yourself. It's your decision whether to patronize them or not.

My father was an atheist. Nonetheless he was an outstanding human being with very high moral codes and was an outstanding member of Legacy. On one occasion he saved a young unmarried mother with kids from being evicted—he had a file and assisted her and others like her for years. The less fortunate! As General Manager of Allied Flour Mills in Sydney he saved many jobs at various flour mills in the industry. Councils were always sending around health inspectors, sniffing around trying to close mills and put people out of work. It was interesting that they had jobs themselves but weren't too worried about the jobs of others—anyway that's how it appeared to me. My father was a very good person. In my opinion, religion and God are personal things and you don't have to go to church to believe in something really special.

There is also nothing wrong with money. I was generous when I had it and I will have it again. When you have money, you can look after your own and others. As you get older you can certainly help more people financially, and particularly your children if you are financially independent. Money is a very good thing if it is used wisely to help in retirement. This system is not available elsewhere and can lead you to financial freedom and wealth quite easily. It requires only limited application and focus to get what you want. If you have money you can help your kids when they really need it.

In my opinion the will is a bit late and families tend to squabble over them. Myself, I wish I had received nothing—in my case the will was simply a divisive instrument which left me with nothing.

* * * * * * * *

Please contact my publisher and I will personally ensure that you are acquainted with full details (subject to signing the privacy form). If you have honest aspirations to succeed in life, you owe it to yourself to at least look at this system. It is no more difficult to get than a conventional loan—these are everywhere. I will repeat again the best use of a loan system is to combine it with your Super and make lots of money in retirement. You will then be able to give the equivalent of your Super to your children.

I have just had an afterthought and will express it. In Life I have found that almost all people are accumulators, especially those who buy a family home. Such types are not foolish with money. If you are foolhardy with money, then perhaps this system is not for you. I have told you about my sole waster in the last 20 years – his type is very uncommon. Home buyers are almost entirely a different breed.

If you want to own your own home outright a lot sooner than with a conventional mortgage. If you want access to cash and a lot of other benefits that are not available with a conventional mortgage. If you are honest, conscientious, an average person and want financial independence. Then, I urge you to give this system a go—it is actually a lot easier to monitor than a conventional loan. In any case, it is entirely your choice—nobody will be twisting your arm. I don't force what I say onto anybody—it's not my style.

Whilst in Brisbane Mark Harris of Home Loan Connexion (HLC) introduced me to an absolutely brilliant marketing person called Jerry C..............; (as a public speaker he was hilarious and had me in stitches at a Home Loan Connexion Christmas party). He developed my system in a real estate format which was never rolled out due to my own financial crisis. His format makes sense, as my system is all about buying heaps of property. It also gives access to cash so that personal loans are a thing of the past. Why have an unsecured personal loan at a much higher interest rate when you can use cash to buy your car. He called it the 'Trebuchet System' which in French means to catapult something. Underneath the letterhead he depicted the words:

FINANCIAL INDEPENDENCE … EARLIER!

A friend of mine, whose opinion I value, asked why I hadn't written the whole book on finance. The real reason is that finance is really quite dry, and I didn't want readers to simply read a couple of pages and toss the book aside (or not buy it). Being a golfer and sports fanatic all my life, I feel the book now has universal appeal and diversity, especially with the final re-print. Finance is bland, and nobody wants to read about the nitty gritty—borrowers just want what they want whether that is a low introductory interest rate, a discounted interest rate for the life of the loan, a split loan, a part-fixed or part-variable loan, flexible repayment options, or perhaps an extended loan term.

This is why there are so many different lenders jockeying for an edge. Banks and other lenders are always tinkering with little things in order to attract more starters (suck them in). Potential borrowers align themselves with a myriad of different lending organisations in the mistaken belief that they are getting something special—they aren't. They are only getting a variation on the same conventional H/L.

Please understand that the conventional H/L is designed to protect the lender—it is structured that way on purpose. The system that I put in place gives you control and is easier to monitor. If you miss a payment with a conventional loan (and your loan is not in advance) the lender will soon let you know. My system avoids loan arrears and gives borrowers the opportunity of paying off their loan in five to six years i.e. they can change their lives for the better and forever. It really is that good!

Existing loans in this country are all structured to protect the lender and in this process the borrower is restrained and gets second best—in other words the lenders don't trust them. I have established many system loans (subject to a signed privacy form) and borrowers take control of their own loan. There is no basis for arrears with a systems loan whereas arrears on a conventional H/L are a different thing. I have forgotten the arrears level associated with normal H/L's but the percentage is quite high (and all the lenders allow for it).

Everybody knows that H/L rates are not fixed, they are variable. Borrowers can fix them but that is always a gamble and don't ask your bank or mortgage broker what to do—they wouldn't have a clue. At the same time there will then be somebody to blame when I/R's do the reverse. We all rely on the governance of The Reserve Bank of Australia (Glenn Steven's honesty is a given). It monitors economic data and sets interest rates independently of the government of the day (irrespective of the tactics applied—governments often try being the bully but it doesn't work). Of far more concern is the major banks not passing on interest rate cuts to their H/L borrowers—this of course is a two edged sword as unhappy borrowers can always jump ship to another bank. My system side-steps any concern about increasing interest rates.

The assessment of genuine savings has long since been a part of establishing eligibility for loan assistance. In the old days genuine savings criteria was adhered to rigidly—akin to today's conventional loan, which has no flexibility. Fundamentally, the bank or other lenders just want to get in and get out unscathed with their profit margin intact.

The buyer has his own perspective. Getting a house in this country is a big step and that commitment is not taken lightly. All lenders take genuine savings into account with the first property. This is not the case with the acquisition of subsequent properties. However banks/lenders are looking to see that there is equity in what is already owned. If a simple refinance to another lender or the purchase of another property is involved, the most common way of financing is through equity. (This is where cross-collateralising comes in—already discussed.) Genuine savings is no longer relevant to this transaction. Whilst it is more relaxed these days I have never been a fan of genuine savings in determining loan eligibility.

Sometimes the borrower involved has far more desire to own a home and because of that he is good at paying his mortgage, but sometimes the borrower who has genuine savings has a mortgage history riddled with arrears. You can have the ridiculous situation of the parents of the borrower's putting in a gift of say $25,000 which if left in a bank account for 3 months is then classed as genuine savings. The borrowers can then be dreadful at repaying the loan. These type of ambiguities are everywhere in the H/L industry.

Despite all the hoo-ha, home loans are both conservative and rigid in this country. Qualifying for a home loan is the same nightmare. (My system is the only alternative to an otherwise "tunnel vision" system—a conventional loan). Loans arrears can appear in the blink of an eye—just lose your job at the wrong time.

In truth, genuine savings doesn't even enter the frame in terms of importance. A borrower can qualify for a large loan (on a small 5% deposit). Following settlement there can be a general downturn in property values. If it is, say, 10%, and the borrower purchased for $400k (current value is $360k) and the loan has just started. The borrower has then effectively lost all their equity i.e. the loan is $380k approximately. In effect their position is worse still—they have negative equity. All of a sudden the borrower can't refinance or sell the property to get out of trouble. If financial difficulty or arrears is added to the equation the borrower is up the proverbial creek without a paddle.

My system gives immunity to everything but fluctuating property values. Not even the government can control property values or negative equity. All the lenders are hoping is that everybody keeps their job and keeps paying their mortgage. If the borrower has one of my systems, negative equity will be of little concern because there will be **no** financial difficulty.

* * * * * * * * *

I must say that nobody goes broke intentionally—I can assure you that I didn't. The journey has always been more important than the destination for me (overcoming the current phase has always been the next thing for me to do). Some people are happy being broke but I'm not one of them. We are all on a journey and I know through experience that my method of home ownership leads to financial freedom and is **definitely the way to go**. I urge all Australians to investigate it thoroughly as there is nothing like it in this country. I was advised by a patent solicitor in Sydney to register my system for protection.

I have something that is really special—it is the only alternative to a totally structured and inflexible Home Loan product in this country. I hope that you the reader and many more Australians are amongst those to use it for their financial betterment.

These remarks relate specifically to benefits listed in this chapter. The benefits in question are those listed as bullet points—have a look yourself and confirm which ones apply. My loan system gives great access to cash and it is this aspect that must be commented on further. Everybody has heard the expression 'cash is king'—well, truer words were never spoken. **The person**

with cash always gets the best deal i.e. with cash you always get the property at the right price (its lowest). Even having a 10% cash deposit can do the trick. You may be looking at a house for $300,000 and get it for $275,000 with a bit of confidence and because you have cash.

A variety of factors can be in play here—most vendors want to sell and will accept less to make it happen, or you can simply find another vendor that is more flexible. As an investor, you don't need to purchase a particular property—if necessary find another property with a vendor that is easier to deal with.

If you are using my system you are buying when everybody is selling (and buying for less is a given when you have cash). I mention that cash can also be taken out to start a business. I have looked at all forms of commercial lending in my time and in almost all cases would recommend against this. Perhaps if you have specialised knowledge and have investigated all aspects thoroughly it might be alright.

I had a friend in the building industry who had a fantastic idea and all of the necessary expertise. Unfortunately, he lost everything (his wife and two lovely daughters) as a result of following his dream at the wrong time (not enough cash)—I am sure that if he had his chance again he would do things differently. This fellow was a good friend of mine and his downfall was hard to take. Kevin was a fully qualified and innovative builder (you should have seen his circular-shaped home!). Please understand his idea was really fantastic but he was short on cash and only young at the time.

I recently saw him on the TV program *The Inventors* with the same idea, properly researched this time—he was in his sixties. He looked like he was finally making a go of it. I am sure Kevin could have kept his family and pursued the idea a little later. In hindsight, it is always easier to know what is best, but I guess it is not always easy at the time. If it was easy nobody would go broke.

Great caution must be exercised if you are starting something new or a new business—cash in large lots usually gets gobbled up. The last thing you want to do is go down the shute with a flagging business or good idea that 'may have worked if'. You really do need that added advantage and knowledge. Young and impetuous is not the answer as they usually end up as the losers.

Don't make the big mistake in thinking you need to reinvent the wheel—ninety-nine times out of a hundred the new business or great idea is not what makes all the money (success is a strange thing). My system is tried and true—it is *not* reinventing the wheel. It can be used by anybody to get ahead rapidly.

In the case of sportsmen perhaps on the fringe of getting into the elite AFL and NRL teams, e.g. like Hawthorn or The Cowboys; those players can make a lot of money in property, which can only take pressure off them as career football players (so that they play better). The players who have made the grade should use my system anyway (to make some more money).

In the case of anybody in the building industry, namely builders, licenced carpenters, plumbers, electricians, and painters—they can use my system as a sideline to make lots of extra money out of property in an industry that they know and already work in. This applies to anybody with a bit of get-up and go—a lot of people have simple carpentry skills as well as knowing what looks good in a room without being a qualified interior decorator, or they can do a garden up. The TV program *Better Homes and Gardens* recently featured a property makeover where the owners made $70K after spending just over

$10K. The property was basic to start with but didn't finish up that way (and the property was subsequently sold at auction).

Anybody with my system will have the cash to do this. All you really need is the desire. Please understand that my system is easier than a conventional loan and makes far more money.

Chapter Three

MY UNIQUE HOME LOAN PRODUCT - A WEALTH CREATING HOME LOAN CONTINUED

I have lost everything twice in my life but at least I've had a go. Once again, I'm having a go – my philosophy is third time lucky. Luck has nothing to do with it! I have a great deal of business experience! In the past it was my job as the Senior Loans Officer in a busy branch in Bourke Street, Melbourne to assess loans for people wanting to go into their own business. I can assure you there are always plenty of starters – there are now and there were then. Some of them undoubtedly don't like working for a boss and want to be their own boss. Statistics are not on the side of new starters however those that make a go of it perhaps second or third time round usually do well – so maybe there's hope for me yet. If you are successful, the rewards are really there – with a job you have a boss and there are always differences of opinion. The pay is never as good when you work for somebody else. The other reason luck has nothing to do with anything is that I had an extremely intelligent father – he had 2 degrees, was an accountant (CPA) for over 60 years and had a photographic memory for words and figures. I am positive the latter is true but will qualify the former by saying that when I was a schoolboy my father quoted great slabs of poetry/Shakespeare that could not have been done without a photographic memory. I don't have his skills but am no dummy all the same. Here is one of life's mysteries. My father was a highly intelligent man yet despite this he had numerous bookings for minor traffic offences. He was always arguing with police when they pulled him over (and he still ended up with all the fines). The law (and road rules) are inflexible. You should always go with the flow – but he didn't. Very strange!

I was born in Toorak, Melbourne and have never been a toff. I started from nothing and always worked hard for what I got. I worked for the CBA and its various entities for 25 years. Finance was always my forte and there wasn't much that I didn't do in that field.

Real estate was on its usual roller-coaster ride in the 80's however one of the perks of working for the CBA in those days was cheap housing finance. I certainly made good use of that facility. My first home was a cheap builder's unit in a very good suburb (Brighton, Melbourne). Whilst experiencing a few nervous moments when selling, it eventually sold. Nervous is an apt description of me at the time, having already signed a long ninety-day contract to purchase another property. I would have been in a real pickle had the Brighton unit not sold when it did. Of course, if you sell first you avoid the risk of a roller-coaster ride yourself. This lesson was learnt when I sold the next property a three storey Terrace house in Hawthorn East. I then purchased a clinker brick home in Harcourt Street, Hawthorn.

What a friendly neighbourhood – my wife (Linda) and I will never forget it. We did a major extension to the property when the kids were little (adding half a house) – thanks to the assistance of the best bricklayer I have ever known. "Con" was his name – I remember making a major deviation to the plans and he just took it in his stride. A record price was obtained for the property when we sold and moved to Queensland.

I suppose everybody has regrets and one of mine is that I wished I had stayed in Melbourne. Greener pastures are not always so green. Whilst decades have passed, that property would now fetch $3M. Nevertheless, I really didn't have a choice at the time based on Queensland plans.

We arrived in Townsville with lots of money and bought a lovely family home that we lived in for 13 years – sometime later we renovated it. A few investment houses were also bought for renovation and resale at a profit, with mixed success. I mortgaged the house and a business was purchased with a large loan from Suncorp Bank i.e. an ice-cream shop named Dal's in the K Mart Plaza. Later a new shop was erected by us and named "Irresistibles" still in the centre of the shopping centre but in a different location. I thought the name selected was great for an ice-cream kiosk and was surprised it wasn't taken by somebody else as a business name.

Just prior to selling the ice-cream shop I undertook a very large development project on the northern edge of Townsville. This involved a subdivision of Mount Kulburn into 40 large housing allotments – all with extensive and long-range views of the sea and Magnetic Island. The subdivision proceeded well at first and became known as "Seaview Park". In fact, that is its name today! The property was owned by my partner's father and his 4 brothers. We established an operating company "Pacific Property P/L" which was funded by me to meet all the expenses. The property itself was acquired through a very clever share purchase (the shareholding of the company). After settlement we owned Frost Industries Ltd and all the land (and there was a lot of that). In the end we got the project finished but it took too long, and the good real estate market was no longer good. We had sold 13 lots during the development stage at good prices but from memory failed to sell a single block at the final Auction, despite a big advertising splurge. Just prior to this I sold the icecream shop at a slight profit and cleared all the company loans. I lost everything else. Thanks to a good Samaritan, my lawyer and a local that I identified in my first book, my family and I continued to live in the house rent fee until I was fortunate enough to repay him.

I will never forget the opportunity lost – in any event it was a very steep learning curve for me.

Finance was certainly my forte and I returned to it. The Queensland State Manager for Aussie Home Loans gave me a chance when I was down and out. I topped the calculator test with the intake (there were about 30 others). I rose to a Senior Consultant with that organisation and received a call from John Symonds (the boss) on reaching a certain milestone in the industry.

I left that organisation when they abolished the $50M trail fee that I had just qualified for. I went to Home Loan Connexion (HLC) – I had previously met the 2 guys that set up HLC (at Aussie). They left a few years before me. Incidentally that organisation has probably been more successful than any other group of finance professionals in the country - it has certainly set all the records in Queensland. From memory I spent over 20 years at HLC and in the last few years was making well over $200K per annum.

At that stage I was marketing my own home loan system to clients and no longer processed any conventional or traditional home loans. I found that clients always had a choice and after seeing my system went with it – a clever wealth creating home loan with so many more benefits.

I made millions from income and what I thought were clever investments only to sacrifice it all because of a family member. The whole thing was made a lot worse when my wife left me. We were separated for 5 years but thank God are now back together. She really is one out of the box.

One may well ask "why have I fallen over again". I took on a partnership and a large commercial undertaking when I was not ready for it (especially with a partner that was calling all the shots). My partner was a highly intelligent and complex character. I came to the opinion that he suffered from diminished public responsibility. I will say no more but it was a view that was shared by others.

Anyway, it was too late, and I was along for the ride like it or not. From experience I have learnt that partnerships rarely work (most lack a common purpose and a few other things). Anyway, life is a great teacher and so is failure. In the other instance I dug a family member out of the gutter and he put me in it – he bled me dry and left me for dead. Mind you, I accept full responsibility for what happened it was me that trusted him. He would have been a pin-prick but for the absence of cash and the GFC.

I was very close to my relation – obviously too close. Helping him and his family get back together with a reasonable life-style was very important to me. This created the vulnerability that I now know brought me down. I was dealing with an unscrupulous character that was play-acting all along. I should have picked the double cross and in fact did 12 months earlier, but my bank were fair-weather friends and the GFC finished me off. **I couldn't sell anything!**

I have been conned twice, but by different parties. If you have been conned twice by the same person then I believe there is something wrong with your mental processes. In the second instance, I suppose my guard was down because it was a family member and a bit further down because it was in fact my older brother. I wasn't going to say anything further about him, but I will. I was fortunate that I was always interested in motivational material whereas my brother's only interest appeared to be rebelling against the system.

He was good at it though and didn't lack courage. He was expelled from Newington College, one of the best school's in Australia. My first book covered some of his exploits. However, I do recall one day at school he stood up in class and challenged his teacher McCrae to come outside for a fight – my brother was 12 and his teacher was an ex rugby player (three times his size). I am not clear about the outcome however my brother's notoriety went all around the school like wildfire. He certainly saw the inside of the headmaster's office (a guy named Pike, and from memory he was one of the best around). I must say though we had some really good times as youngsters and later when we were older. The golfing episodes when we were 9 and 10 were hilarious - they were recanted in my first book. Feedback from golf professionals and others all around the country was fantastic. My brother and I had a fantastic meal at a German beer restaurant close to the Manly ferry on my last trip to Sydney. I think it was the last time I saw him!

My brother left home when he was 14 and lived on his wits until he was an adult. Later, he became a street fighter (formidable) and was mixed up in other bad things. On the plus side he was a natural sportsman. The only thing that held him back was his temper. He had an anger management problem (11 out of 10) which I am sure stopped him from being a world class tennis player. As it was he was an LTAA Tennis coach at 63 – amicably teaching young kids just starting off and thrashing advanced tennis players in the amateur ranks.

I suppose my brother was a natural truant if there is such a thing – an absentee from life. He was an arty type as a youngster and a very talented painter (using water or oil). I suspect that he felt cornered as an adolescent as it simply wasn't kosha to have his kind of aspirations in the 1960's. Part of the problem of course was that he only wanted to do what **he** wanted to do – if it was main-stream he railed against it almost immediately. I think my mother hated him to the grave! It was different with my father – I think he always believed there was a good side to my brother. My father was very eloquent and kept my brother out of jail on one occasion (representing him in court). A trumped-up charge by a senior sergeant of police would have stuck had it not been exposed for what it was by my father.

Shackelford's are from a line of long livers (most have made 100). But, by my reckoning he was approx. 30 years short of that benchmark.

In his late 60's he contracted the most progressive form of brain cancer. I used to visit him quite often in the Royal North-shore Hospital. He was opened up but the cancer was found to be in-operable - Chemotherapy normally knocks the body around but he managed to walk vast distances afterwards. He was like Superman, astonishing willpower!

My brother died last December from what I believe was a break down in his immune system (that let the cancer back in).

Perhaps his death was sudden otherwise, I am sure that he would have called me. All I can say now is, what a waste!

I can't help thinking he was rudderless i.e. if you aim at nothing you hit nothing. A dreamer is in a different world but if you think something is possible, I am sure you are half way there. Having a goal! I never saw that side of my brother really. He worked for the ABC for a few years, was a single figure golfer and got to a very high standard at Tennis.

My brother could have done anything, but he never did. Whilst his willpower was exceptional I believe the subconscious mind is the way to achieve things in life i.e. the power of the mind. My brother wouldn't have known who Napoleon Hill was (he could have been a bus-driver for all he knew).

When my father was just starting off with The Ford Motor Co the whole family went to Canada/America. We lived in the Prince Edward Hotel in Ontario just across The Michigan River (Detroit U.S.A) for 6 months. As kids we got up to some terrible pranks. Detroit was a dangerous place but there was a tunnel under the river which we took on several holidays to America. In winter the river would ice over, and you wouldn't have to be Einstein to guess where we were. Out on the river! It's a wonder my brother and I didn't finish at the bottom of the river. We stayed in Canada about 2.5 years.

I have talked about my brother for 3 reasons. We were close, and the money thing should never have happened. He was a wayward bloke at least in my mind and a person that could have been so much more. We all need to do something with our lives and set goals even if they seem unachievable (because you never know).

Goals in the home ownership area are important to all Australians. With my system you can raise your sights i.e. pay down home loan debt in record time, raise your living standards, drive and own new cars more frequently and reach financial stability a lot earlier etc. Home ownership is part of the Australian Culture – probably more so than any other country on earth. My system is ready made and will help everyone achieve their goals. **Whatever they are!**

I am now going to say what I think is more important than anything else: mistakes and failure are a part of life. Often the greatest success will follow a failure. The reason that I have told you about my failures is that I have had some great successes.

In my case, I firmly believe that it has all happened for a reason and the best is yet to come. I simply have another goal or goals!

Anyway, I have always been able to make money. It must be a core belief of mine! If lots of money is just around the corner I will undoubtedly soon find out?

I have always read a great deal and when I was a young-man I was crazy about motivational books. The question for me was always "why is one guy jumping out of himself and the next a blob." My favourite book was" Think and Grow Rich" released in the United States of America by Napolean Hill early in the 20th century. I believe Melvin Powers released a far more palatable version of the book a century later. It was a sensation in the USA and went straight into the best seller lists. I have mislaid my copy however a fresh copy was bought in Caloundra about 9 years ago. All the great men in history have achieved that status i.e. greatness, through the common principles of goal setting and visualisation.

Everybody has something or things they really want. I believe that it is essential to **write** them all down, prioritise there achievement (in order of importance to you) and most importantly set a **deadline** for achieving the goal. If something is no longer a goal remove it from your list.

Visualisation and positively worded statements help us all achieve our goals.

We all have the brain power to achieve what we really want in life. If you want something badly it is also important to **never give up** - in his book Napoleon Hill deals with this very topic in depth (citing instances of people giving up just prior to achieving what they set out to do, with others taking over and achieving the success that they should have had themselves).

It is important to realise that we all have different priorities. My system is like goal setting – there are so many good outcomes possible it is important to determine what you want. With a conventional loan you get the family home and a loan repayable over 3 decades (4 years less if you pay fortnightly) and that is all you get. There are no goals to set other than keeping a little in front with the loan if you can, just in case misfortune strikes. A conventional home loan is only designed for what I have said, whereas my home loan system is entirely different and better.

Multiple goals can be achieved at the one time and it gets the house too.

Here is another of Life's mysteries which I feel I must mention. I am the uncle of a guy that has been to jail for drug possession - he was also a user. He was gifted $5M by his girlfriend and now lives the life of Riley without the girlfriend. Life really does deliver some surprises!

The same Conventional home loan is on the market after 50/60 years. It does the job it was designed for – it gets the house and **nothing more**. I believe it has been universally accepted in this country for one reason and only one reason i.e. there has never been a viable alternative until **now**. I wrote conventional loans for 15 years and I've had a very long career in finance. In the past 25-30 years I have **exclusively** processed my home loan systems i.e. I have done both. That is why I **know** that my wealth creating H/L is immeasurably better for the man in the street.

I will repeat that I am a finance broker that has marketed **all** the different home loans that have ever existed. Please don't delude yourself - **they are all basically the same**. The differences in the CBA, NAB, Westpac, Suncorp home loans aren't worth talking about. They are all basically the same. I am not knocking those loans they have always achieved the collective purpose of home ownership. My system does all that but has so many other benefits that you can tap into after settlement – you certainly don't get them with a conventional home loan from a bank (the bank manager is a thing of the past with my system).

I want to digress a little before winding up. Let's return to the aspect of people achieving what they want (their goals). It is a subject that has fascinated me all my life. The book "Think and Grow Rich" has been a bible to me all my life. It really is a no nonsense and practical way of achieving all that you want in life. A good friend of mine recently gave me a book to read "The Answer" by Allan and Barbara Pease. I was a bit sceptical at first however, having read the book believe it is just as inspiring as the other novel I have referred too, especially the last 2 chapters – certainly recommended reading for anybody that wants to get ahead in life.

This might sound corny, but I believe life is a gift and what I have been given is a "gift from God". My most important job is ensuring that my home loan system is readily available and used throughout this great country. Home ownership is truly sacrosanct i.e. every Australians heritage. After-all, a Conventional loan is everywhere (institutionalised).

Do you want your own home? Do you want to take control and make all the decisions? Do you want to repay home loan debt in your time-frame (say 5 years)? Do you want access to cash? Your own wages! Do you want to purchase investment properties before and after retirement? Do you want to multiply your superannuation benefit so that you can give the equivalent of your Super to your kids? Do you want to drive new cars and turn them over every ¾ years? If you operate a business do you want to use turnover to reduce the home loan interest you pay?

No more high interest rate loans.

There is more information on my website which I believe is now live: www.wealthvantagehomeloans.com.au

I have said that each investment is isolated with my system. Well I can assure you that it is **not** isolated if you use a bank (remember a bank manager always has 2 hats even if he is a nice guy).

There is a Royal Commission into the banks and not just because they make obscene profits. Unfortunately, we are learning that dishonest dealings go to the core of the financial system. Large and powerful corporations are involved – it will be interesting to see if there is **any permanent change in their behaviour** i.e. human beings ripping off other human beings in the name of the mighty $. It seems to me that large corporations simply don't care enough about the individual, especially the banking one's. Part of the reason that profits are so high is that banks are tough on borrowers. This toughness is no doubt related to profitability – corporations are listed on the Stock Exchange. Shareholders are the real owners of the business. The listed price of shares can be markedly affected by profitability/dividends and other trading factors. This is a sad state of affairs! My system is about evening up the playing field for the borrower, so he gets a fair go – he's not getting that right now.

After 5/6 decades there is NOW an alternative to a conventional home loan.

An alternative that is a million times better and "tried and true" over 30 years. I have been in a finance all my working life i.e. a career spanning almost 52 years.

A smart person realises that he doesn't have to re-invent the wheel to get ahead in life – use my home loan system to achieve what you want.

Every Australian should see this system and make their own decision to be financially independent – it is never too late.

Refinances, purchases – the system home loan caters for them all.

Chapter Four

COMMERCIAL

I was heavily involved in commercial finance at the CBA (Commonwealth Bank of Australia). My start in finance was with that bank some 45 years ago when I was the Senior Loans Officer in an elite Bourke Street branch in Melbourne. From memory I spent almost 15 years handling complex Commercial applications. Everything from loans to politicians, doctors, dentists, an untold number of people purchasing businesses, large building contractors, a Jewish textile manufacturer named Dascal (a man of great energy who I will never forget. He was also one of the smartest and most successful business men I have ever met) and many others. Dascal's two sons inherited a very successful business. On a recent trip to Melbourne I touched base with one of the sons. If they are half as shrewd as their father I am sure the family business is still thriving. Actually, it must be OK – I had coffee with one of the son's, and his house was large and very comfortable in a leafy and expensive location close to the City.

When I arrived at Chancery House branch I was a H/L specialist, having been in that role at seven different inner City branches – the longest stint of 2/3 years was at Collingwood branch. From memory I shifted to Chancery House from Northcote – my appointment was as the branches Home Loan officer. This role lasted for a couple of years but changed dramatically following the sudden death of the permanent manager Clive Mander. A Senior relieving manager Lester Langley arrived as his replacement.

I found myself doing a mixture of Commercial and Home Loan work - about two years later all of it was Commercial.

The Senior Loans Officer was promoted out and his replacement who spent approximately 2 years in the role resigned (incidentally he was a great operator who left to drive trucks in his own business – a guy by the name of Alan Freeman). He told me why he really left.

As a result of all these events I was thrust into the role of Senior loans Officer doing Commercial loan applications solely. This involved some penciling for Lester who was still the relieving manager. He was a big guy with a big heart and a huge capacity to help others including me – a part-time job with a stockbroker was directly attributable to him (his brother was a director of Western Mining Corporation). Because of his gregarious nature and other qualities he saw most of the customers himself – churning out submissions as fast as clients left his office.

Chancery House Branch occupied the first two stories of a 17 storey building in Bourke Street, Melbourne. Of course, that building was demolished years later to make way for the new RACV building that is now its Head Office in Victoria.

Lester Langley was my boss and also the Branch manager. I must say that he really was the best boss I ever had and an absolutely champion bloke. He was also a kindred spirit and a golfer and a member of Riversdale Golf Club where I was fortunate enough to have won a few Championships. There was a fierce rivalry between us on the table tennis table in the staff room upstairs (so much so that I later got a championship table tennis table of my own at home). We also went on lunches with a few branch clients that we both dealt with.

A very hot blooded Italian named Nino Cocivera took Lester and me out to lunch as reciprocation for Lester's largess in approving another loan for a development project of his. To be fair Nino's work had real appeal—not just street appeal. He was a renowned Italian builder (both emotional and flamboyant at the same time). All his work and finishes were spectacular right down to the paint jobs on doors, i.e. no brush marks and you could see your own reflection like a mirror. A flawless finish! He was one of our best clients and a very clever guy. If he couldn't get the required area and block of dirt that he wanted he would just walk away. It was the best restaurant in South Yarra (very snobby). For the first time I had the real Italian Minestrone soup and it was exquisite. Nino did large scale strata developments in all the good areas, i.e. Hawthorn, Camberwell, South Yarra and Brighton. He worked hard and really put in and deserved his wealth. All of his projects were fantastic and everything sold. The builder's profit is always tied up in the last few sales—prices were never heavily discounted (such was the quality of his work).

The other guy I am compelled to mention was Philip Dascal, a Jewish client who wined and dined Lester and I. Actually, I think he was the smartest businessman I have ever met. He was the only borrower who made money out of a Swiss Franc Loan and it was a big one. I am mystified how he knew the secret—everybody knew the loans were real cheap interest-wise. The trick with Foreign Currency Loans was always when to take one out. CBA were lucky, they didn't do many Foreign Currency Loans (FCL's).

Dascal knew that with FCL'S it was all determined by the get in exchange rate. If the rate is too high you don't entertain an un-hedged Foreign Currency Loan. You simply walk away. Anyway he got a good rate going in and a lower rate on repayment, (which you must get or you are dead in the water). How he knew this was always a mystery to me. He was a very wealthy Jew, and probably a long time dead as he was old when I was twenty-nine.

I asked him one day why he had no bad debts or any provisions, (he had a corporate setup) and he simply said "I don't have any bad debts because I don't sell textiles to anybody who doesn't pay". He imported everything, and would have handed over an extremely healthy Textile business to his two married sons, (whom I met). I had a great relationship with Philip Dascal. He took me and Lester to Vlado's Steak House in Bridge Road, Richmond. All you could eat was meat. His steaks were legendary and were always referred to as the best in the country. You could only have delicious strawberry pancakes for dessert (I did). Dascal told us in advance not to eat for a week. Old Vlado has passed away but the business trades on after seventy years—it is still called Vlado's, at the same location. The steak must still be fantastic.

My father was one of the big bosses for The Ford Motor Company overseas - I had about 15 new GT falcons to drive while he was away. When the deal ran out I bought the last GT falcon at a dis-count (a V8 with a wild cam) and traded it in on a red Lamborghini Urraca (it had a v8 in the back). Jesus! It could go!

I must say that Lester really was the greatest human being! And I reckon he was the only bloke that would have let me park the red monster in the undercover park in the basement. He was a real gentleman in every sense of the word – I will never forget him.

Lester eventually shifted on and was replaced by another Senior Manager, Kevin Ryan. Kevin and Lester were the same mould really both excellent delegators and Balance Sheet Lenders. Old school but very smart! I was very fortunate to have them as Senior managers – the learning curve was colossal.

My time under Kevin Ryan was short. I was shifted sideways (not promoted) to Branch Lending Department at 367 Collins Street (next to The Stock Exchange). This was a whole new ball game! I was exposed to all forms of lending and related matters – all the administrative stuff that branches could not approve themselves or stuff they had approved but needed sanctioning on. I processed lots of things to a Senior Manager named Murray Columbine who was feared by most. Murray was an explosive character but highly intelligent and invariably right.

As a young-man I had an acute lack of confidence. Ron Thomas, The Manager for Victoria, was a real mentor to me both in the bank and on the golf course. I would never have entered The Amateur Championship of Australia at Victoria nor done anything else with the golf only for him. He became a staunch friend and ally.

Whilst in Branch Advances department I was exposed to lending to Housing Co-operatives, Pencilling for Ron Thomas and other Senior Managers on larger

Commercial Applications and Foreign Currency Loans (FCL's). I finished up doing loans in Swizz Francs and Japanese Yen. The Dascal from Chancery House days had a large FCL in Swiss Francs that he did very well with. After a while I did all the processing on his file to Murray Columbine. While I mentioned these matters in my first book they did have a profound effect on me. As a young man it engendered a dislike for many things that banks do. Today and in general they don't seem to care a lot about individuals. The old Bank of NSW was good at selling up farmers in the 1970's and they did that with gay abandon. This back fired on them when they were shown to be totally incompetent with Un-hedged Swizz Franc Loans (and farmers got a reprieve). My dislike is now more intense as Westpac has been exposed once more in The Royal Commission for its unsavoury sell-up tactics with farmers (a bit of déjà vu)

As banks get bigger and their profitability increases, shareholders have a greater say and easily override issues pertaining to social conscience. Shareholders like profits so social conscience issues don't seem to matter that much – I think the Royal Commission has really focused on trust issues with all of The Big 4 Banks – most people have trust issues (even those that take out loans). After-all, banking is not rocket science. All they do is get a whole lot of money in fixed deposits, saving and cheque accounts, etc. (depositors balances) and lend that out at a higher rate. The Big 4 Banks are especially good at it and I can assure you that they are in all the lucrative areas. Home and commercial lending attracts fire insurance over houses and factories, businesses and provides gravy train revenue streams with virtually no claims. Banks are also now selling other products namely their own investments, life insurance etc. They are now in areas that have been the domain of other financial institutions. I believe it's all a bit scary with banks and others having the attitude that anything that generates a buck is acceptable. As long as it is profitable! That's all shareholders care about, bigger and better profits.

Everybody wants a loan. The problem is that I have been involved in the provision of every loan type there is. Sometimes a loan is the answer, but not always. In the banking world I believe it is more and more a numbers game. A home loan is OK when it gets you the house but if you lose your job at the wrong time and lose the house (and your family) you won't think much of the home loan. Similarly, if you take out a commercial loan and the business goes under because you are short of working capital you are not going to be thinking how great the business loan was. The fact is the borrower is expected to allow for every possible contingency. It is his fault if something goes wrong! Where would we all be if nobody took a risk. There would be considerably less houses and there are millions of them. There would also be considerably less businesses in private enterprise. Obviously, there is an abundance of both, proving that human beings are resilient and will always have a go i.e. some of the most successful people in history come from the poorest backgrounds. Remember though a loan is just a loan. There should be less risk but The Big 4 Banks make Billions now and I don't think they want to change anything – a fairer system is irrelevant to them. We are not all accountants or financial experts. In any event there are plenty of them that get into trouble financially.

The real truth is that risk and reward always have to be manageable. I have a system in both the Housing and Commercial areas where this is the case. The borrower can forge his own future, attain financial independence with no concern that the bank will sell him up. Most importantly the borrower has 100% control (the existing system is the reverse).

Banks hold a first mortgage – that's all they are interested in holding (especially if the loan is a reasonable size). The Bank takes no risks, they are left for the borrower. Borrowers that make a go of it are left alone and those that flounder are sold up. With a more responsible lending system (like mine) more people would survive and make a decent living.

In all cases the borrower signs the mortgage – if not the loan is declined. The mortgage document has already been discussed but only in the housing area. A mortgage document in the Commercial area is NO different (it must be signed too).

If there is NO financial difficulty a signed mortgage document will never be used against a borrower in the Commercial or Home Loan area. The only exception might be if the lender or bank is privy to criminal or illegal activity.

The benefits of my system in the Commercial area are similar to those in the Home Loan area. In fact you will have a new and far better experience with this home loan facility by virtue of the sheer number of homes. **My system H/L is not just a LOAN!** You can't have a Commercial system if you don't have a Commercial property. Simple logic! A Commercial loan or one of my systems in the Commercial area can only be secured by a mortgage over Commercial property. In other words the property has to be zoned Commercial. There is a distinct advantage in a Commercial loan system when you want to buy a business and its freehold or an existing factory i.e. a commercial property. The security for the loan is a registered first mortgage over a Commercially zoned block.

Imagine you are purchasing a large retail tyre business (including freehold) for $2.6M. My Housing system gives spectacular access to cash however input of $2.6M in cash is simply too much to drag out of anything. And that would miss out on all the tax advantages (and there are too many to ignore).

The better alternative is to put in a reduced cash amount of say $800K and borrow the remaining $1.8M against goodwill and the value of the freehold. If profitability stacks up they (the banks) will go to 80% on the freehold value plus a bit extra for the goodwill – this should qualify the borrower for a 15 year term and a good interest rate.

* * * * * * * *

There are a few borrowers that want to own their own commercial premises. This can comprise an office building, the aforementioned tyre business, or a factory or a warehouse. Actually, I will use an office building as an example as this highlights why commercial finance is essential for the borrower. **Whilst my H/L system is great for getting cash** – in this case the amount of cash required is too much. Also the substantial tax and depreciation allowances demand that a commercial loan facility be used:

BUILDING – 6 STOREYS

Purchase price $2,600,000   building

Less   800,000   Cash deposit

                       $1,800,000   Commercial loan

The borrower operates his own business from the ground floor and sublets the remaining 5 floors. Almost all of the loan is tax deductible. Actually, if the owner of the building operates his own business from the ground floor and there is a rent back arrangement he can effectively claim the lot on tax. As I have already said there is no tax claim (perhaps the deposit) with my housing system but an enormous one commercially. Too big to ignore!

There are a large number of applications effecting R/E, retail and motor industries in commercial and other areas. A borrower with a conventional commercial loan will retire debt over a 15 year term or slightly less. One of my commercial systems will see it disappear in say 5 years especially if the borrower has my H/L system as well. The borrower can use one of my commercial systems to settle the transaction as illustrated in the diagram.

None of the substantial tax advantages etc. can be accessed unless a commercial facility is used. THE BORROWER MUST EMBRACE A COMMERCIAL LOAN i.e. a normal commercial loan or better still one of my commercial systems for the transaction.

In Australia housing is by far the greatest requirement. There are a massive number of houses and therefore mortgages spread around the edges of a very large land mass. By comparison there is a smaller number of businesses. However, one feeds off the other –look at the shops and businesses in the various suburbs let alone large Cities like Perth, Adelaide, Melbourne, Sydney and Brisbane. In Melbourne City alone the sheer number of high rise buildings and businesses is staggering. **This is the domain of the commercial lender.**

The best use of my H/L system is when it is used in conjunction with my commercial system. A borrower that shifts into the commercial area has invariably been successful in the housing arena. He might have paid off his house! He might have a string of investment properties! He might have a lot of cash and want to put it to work! The important thing is that he will already be aware of his ability to move into the commercial area i.e. own his own building and operate his own business as per the previous example. **This will only happen though if the borrower has the desire to own a commercial freehold. Many don't! Many that operate businesses are happy having a landlord and paying rent.** Also if you are buying commercial you can't always get the right location.

Having purchased a commercial freehold using one of my commercial systems the borrower can then use my H/L system to help get the debt down quicker.

At the outset the borrower owes a large amount i.e. $2M dollars. He will be keen to reduce his exposure and his debt. Clearly he will have access to a lot of rent plus funds from his business plus tax and other benefits to meet repayments. My commercial system involves a holding account! **Using both systems is the ideal way for a borrower to reduce his loan term dramatically. And get a better overall result.**

There are many other instances where my commercial system can benefit the borrower i.e. in lieu of a conventional commercial loan re additional working capital, machinery, commercial vehicles, a shop-fit, re-stock etc. If a commercial system is taken out the debt component can be paid off quickly using the approach recommended in the previous paragraph.

* * * * * * * *

Remember Conventional Loans whether Housing or Commercial are just loans. Conventional loans by nature do not look after everybody only some. Let's be honest if a commercial borrower goes broke due to a shortage of working capital he will not be praising the **commercial loan** that got him the business in the first place.

Failure is a great learning curve! I have proven that results are better for everybody when the borrower is in control – he is in control with my system but not necessarily with a loan i.e. the risk is far more manageable.

Whilst there is only one or two financial institution that still provide the machinery for my system commercially, that's all that is necessary! My system is alive and well in the commercial area i.e. borrowers can benefit from both systems (H/L and Commercial).

There are many instances where shop owners are happy paying rent. i.e. with no desire to own. Shopping Centres, shops on group titles, individual shops and factories, factory-ettes and the old-fashioned shopping strips etc. are all examples of this. Industrial estates can operate on the same basis i.e. say TNT has a purpose built facility on a large block where the owner is a commercial landlord. Estates like these proliferate all large cities. Shopping complexes are everywhere and operate on exactly the same basis.

Almost all people that operate small businesses pay **rent i.e. rent is one of their most important expenses.**

Only a small number of entrepreneurs will own their own premises or want to. As I have already said my H/L system can be beneficial to **any entrepreneur** establishing or operating a business irrespective of the rent he pays. Access to cash is important to every business. And the process of putting it in and taking it out is made easy with both of my systems. A restaurant is a good example. Let's look at that! An owner can be facing outlays for lighting, tables and chairs, display cabinets, ovens, microwaves, freezers cutlery, linen and a host of other items. All of this commercial equipment can be financed via a commercial system. All the data can then be catalogued for the borrowers accountant prior to him completing tax and other returns for the business.

The aforementioned applies to **every business.** Shopping Centres are a good example i.e. Coles, Woolworths, Big W, Target, Myers, David Jones, Best and Less, coffee shops, dress shops etc. etc. Anything that is the domain of a shop-fitter! There are many other applications.

Whilst there is a smaller demand for purchase of commercial freeholds it is still there. I had an entrepreneurial person that purchased a large shop on one title. She subdivided it into two smaller shops for the two rentals she would get. I remind you that there is an army of trading banks and commercial lenders out there ready to assist with business requirements. Obtaining a small overdraft is a good example, say $20,000. The arithmetic for a simple one might be as follows: house value $300,000 conventional home loan $200,000 overdraft $20,000 i.e. this is plenty of straight security cover for any commercial lender. The usual conditions apply: a commercial interest rate, the balance is normally expected to fluctuate in and out of credit and the facility is reviewed annually. Second mortgage security is normally acceptable! I have an alternative way of doing the above that might be more useful.

My only priority is to see Australians using my H/L system. On the odd occasion this will create the need for my system commercially.

My commercial system is a lot better than a commercial loan however it is still a commercial facility. For that reason, it will attract an interest rate that is automatically higher than any residential facility, separate commercial security and a maximum 15 year term (clear in 3-5 years with my system).

Remember though to access one of my commercial systems you must take **title** to the property. And that can only be over a commercially zoned property.

I am sure you will enjoy the concluding chapter – it is all about the borrower taking control and him benefiting in so many other ways – life enhancing ways.

Conclusion

Generally, finance brokers don't help with costs. I am broke due to my own circumstances however I have different priorities - money is not the driving force it used to be. As a finance broker, I made lots of money and lots of money out of my own system so that is why I will initially do my best to assist with costs. In the past I have always paid for the valuation report (one of the borrower's major expenses). As things develop this may still be the case but initially I will be committed to paying a referral fee to an army of referrers. I have no doubts this will get things moving.

The broker that is just starting off, or a normal broker with only traditional product at his disposal has intense competition to face in writing good business i.e. there are literally thousands of Conventional loans on the market. I firmly believe that selling a conventional loan is hard-work. The broker must convince ASIC (Australian

Securities and Investment Commission) as well as the customer regarding his loan choice. Selling the facility is both hard-work and hard-fought so it is not surprising that most if not all brokers prefer to keep their commission intact.

I have an excellent record with loan approvals. However, if a loan is declined due to the absence of full disclosure I will not be paying any costs i.e. a lot of work is done for nothing. An application fee if paid is always refunded by a lender (bank) when a loan is declined. Nobody is reimbursed for work done. Obviously, lenders like to keep declined loans to an absolute minimum.

I can't ever remember processing marginal loans. However, I can certainly remember getting many conventional home loan approvals including home loans using my system. They were always for needy applicants and people who I believe deserved H/L assistance. Actually, I also processed a couple of 100% LVR loans and they were also approved. These home loans were for applicants with **NO equity** i.e. the loans were for the full purchase price of the house property. The applicants had to be able to service the loan and still have to come up with the conveyancing cost (solicitor's legal fee) and pay a hefty mortgage insurance premium. But you could still do the loan if you could prove **servicing.** In fact servicing became the only real loan criteria.

Of course these loans disappeared when the big crash in 100% loans happened in the USA. Every finance broker in this country will remember the crash in America – it was enormous. It heralded a virtual collapse of the home loan market in that country. Houses and residential real estate were being purchased everywhere in the mistaken belief that values would continue to go through the roof (up). Initially, the huge demand fuelled an increase in values but this bubble burst via some normal economic turn of event. All of a sudden those people with some equity saw it disappear and those that took out 100% loans had no equity at all – and worse still had no prospect of having any equity. **Prices were falling!** From memory they were free-falling and making a mess of the home loan system in that country.

The expression LVR used in the ensuing paragraphs means loan to value ratio.

If something happens in the USA there is usually a fall-out in Australia. In this instance the fall-out for us was the disappearance of 100% LVR home loans. They disappeared over night! For me, this high-lighted a fundamental difference between us and the USA at least in the home loan area. I can't talk for the USA, but the 100% loan was hard to get in Australia. Applicants had to clearly demonstrate servicing. I am pretty sure that the 100% loans processed by me had no arrears – perhaps servicing criteria was more stringent here. I am sure it was. In other words the people that took out 100%LVR home loans would have kept their properties and would today have equity. Of course they may well have sold and realised some equity. The so-called "crash" was a few years ago.

I believe that the 95% LVR loan itself (applicants with only 5% deposit for the purchase of a house) is now harder to get as a result of what happened in the USA. Obviously, the abolition of 100% LVR loans would also have had the same effect.

The traditional deposit for a home loan in this country is 10% and you will also need this for one of my system home loans i.e. a 90% Lending margin. Applicants cannot get a 95% LVR home loan with my system. There are however many ways that people with only 5% deposit can work towards it. I am happy to talk to anybody about how they can create additional equity – without thinking to hard there are 2 ways of doing this. If you have a 5% deposit for a house you want to buy, just go ahead and buy it using a conventional 95% LVR housing loan. That way you can still purchase the house of your dreams or the one you really want at the time. Buy the house first and create the equity later. I can process the conventional 95% LVR home loan for you at the outset and convert it later when the equity is right – conversion to one of my home loans will be worth the wait. **It will change and improve your live forever!**

Government Agencies such as APRA (Australian Prudential Regulation Authority) act to protect the financial interests of the inhabitants of this country. Those organisations have also been involved in the recent Royal Commission into Australia's financial institutions – AMP and the Major Banks. All of these institutions provide a multitude of financial products including conventional home loans.

My system home loan enables ordinary Australians (the man in the street) to access financial independence that is quite out of reach with the current loan offering. My system also provides scope for improvement in the life-style of borrowers and many other benefits which are extremely important to them (these benefits are listed in a prior chapter of this book). The wholesale purchase of property by Australians i.e. the family home and further investment properties is facilitated by my system. The existing home loan does not facilitate this on any reasonable scale. My system opens the door for Australians to be better off and purchase residential property on a much larger scale than is currently possible.

The aforementioned government agencies including APRA control investment lending by Foreign Nationals and many other things, so that conditions for purchase of prime residential R/E by Australian Citizens can be optimised – this is what my system is all about. **Australians buying more of our real estate!**

There are two broad categories that make up all income earners in Australia. Only individuals from one of these groups can take out a loan as they are the only ones with the capacity to repay it. The loan can be for any purpose i.e. commercial, housing or personal etc. On the one hand you have the PAYG income earner or employee that works for a business entity of some description. That can be an individual earning a fly in fly out income or your typical mom and dad that join together and make up the vast majority of H/L's approved and settled in this country. Then there is the self-employed (S/E) entity which can be an individual, a corporation, a limited liability company, a Public Company listed on the Stock Exchange, an ordinary Pty Ltd Company and any number of other business entities. Again, the vast majority of businesses are probably operated by moms and dads all over the country using Pty Ltd companies (those companies also get home loans).

Don't hold me to the exact date, but back in the early eighties loans were introduced to help self-employed clients borrow money. Businesses/Firms across Australia had always provided work for lots of Aussies but in many instances the owners couldn't borrow themselves. It is my belief that the Lo Doc Loan came along for this reason. Clearly, there was a big gap in the market. Prior to Lo Doc lending you always used to hear "How do we lend to people operating their own business?" Often business operators would not have the mandatory 2 years results (mainly profit and loss statements) to satisfy full document status. The culprit was in fact the requirement for 2 years figures. It was a strict requirement of the full document loan facility in which full evidence of income proved servicing. However, in all other instances clients could access taxable income details and this became the basis for the new Lo Doc loan. The Lo Doc Loan was a game changer. You still had to satisfy loan servicing by inserting taxable income in the declaration but it **did** solve the basic problem for many S/E people (they could borrow just like everybody else). Unfortunately, there was some dreadful weaknesses in the new documentation. Eventually ASIC got involved and procedural and documentation changes fixed all the problems i.e. brokers could no longer sign off on Lo Doc declarations and the sign off on taxable income shifted to the client's accountant. Before this the taxable income insertion in Lo Doc declarations opened the door to the worst form of abuse. Shady mortgage brokers (and clients) and bank branches and other organisations with input clerks probably weren't even aware of the abuse that was taking place. I am sure that inflated taxable income particulars would have been inserted to get loans approved. This in itself would not necessarily have incurred the wrath of applicants for they probably didn't know the declaration was wrong. Certainly mortgage brokers acting independently of their clients, would not have had a job if they had been exposed – the likelihood of that was extremely low. Please understand the real problem was not dishonesty but the lax document everybody was using. Clearly, the taxable income insertion should always have been signed off by the clients accountant. On a positive note however, just about every lender had a Lo Doc product that could be accessed. However, if you wanted a Lo Doc Loan there was a bit of a sting in the tail – borrowings were generally restricted to 60% of the value of freehold security (first mortgage). In my mind this was a simple case of lenders collectively hedging their bets. In other words if they were going to accept loan servicing on the borrowers say so, then it was fair to lower the lending margin against available security and thereby reduce the likelihood of potential losses. The S/E applicant still had to have full financials to be considered for the full document loan i.e. 80% LVR loans and possibly higher with lenders mortgage insurance (LMI).

Nevertheless, Lo Doc Loans were taken up and were very popular for business operators despite the larger deposit i.e. 40%.

As Lo Doc lending got more prevalent there were a number of lenders that were prepared to approve loans on a higher margin (above 60% LVR). I was aware of a Major Bank that used a combination of financial information plus other Lo Doc criteria to lend at the 60% margin.

In many ways, I saw Lo Doc lending (in the eighties) as the saviour of self-employed business operators. At the same time there is little doubt that Lo Doc loans were abused by all and sundry including borrowers. In my opinion this was due to document deficiency as much as anything else.

In the early days, a mortgage broker could sign off on a Lo Doc deal even his own. This practice is no longer acceptable (ASIC stopped it). ASIC now heavily polices many aspects of the Finance Industry including all Credit Licences. I think this is a good thing!

I have a corporate set up where my company holds an Australian Credit Licence number 387789 and I am the sole director of the company. **I take nothing for granted.**

My approach has always been an honest one. When ASIC assumed control of finance and the mortgage broker there was a mass exodus from the industry - many dishonest practices also disappeared.

Whilst a self-employed borrower must sign off a Lo Doc loan it is also mandatory for his accountant to sign off on taxable income. That taxable income will then tell the lender if he can afford the loan – if the lender is still not satisfied (very rare) he can still request evidence of income. Collusion between a borrower and his accountant is too risky these days especially in the event of **exposure.**

In the early days there were no safe guards. There were plenty of desperate mortgage brokers and others prepared to quote anything they were told (without checking). A dishonest system! This would have been unacceptable to some brokers and others who may have done a lot of work and wanted the commission. In my mind it is always better to be honest and check taxable income at the outset, **as the end NEVER justifies the means.**

I was a Lo Doc specialist and wrote many H/L facilities (using my system) with all of the banks including the Majors. It was standard procedure for me to obtain physical confirmation of the borrower's taxable income from his accountant before completing the declaration. I had a special relationship with The B/D/M of Macquarie Bank and established many Lo Doc Loans with that organisation. As far as I know there were never any bad debts.

Macquarie is a non-retail bank. Non-retail banks don't have depositor's balances so they can't lend against them like the Big 4 Major Banks. Depositor balances include funds in cheque accounts, savings accounts, fixed or term deposits etc. Suncorp is a retail bank and as such has its own lending percentage against depositor's balances.

There were many abuses of the Lo Doc loan in the early days. It had no safeguards like today! **I believe the abuse was fully exploited!**

A Lo Doc loan is where a client (the borrower) does not prove servicing. In other words, a declaration is simply signed stating that repayments are affordable. In the old days the borrower signed the declaration and the rest of the form was signed off by a finance department handling the matter or sometimes a local bank branch or manager or mortgage broker depending on who the client was dealing with.

Without doubt the most high profile case of abuse was Storm Financial. That organisation was well on its way to becoming Australia wide when the GFC hit. It came crashing down! As I understand the situation,

Cassimatus (the owner and founder) was aided and abetted by one of the Major Banks.

Many of the investors in Storm Financial were pensioners on very low Centrelink incomes. They might have been guilty of seeking an un-realistic return (itself a form of greed) however they did not deserve the out and out dishonesty and rorting that occurred.

I had a good idea what Storm was doing on the Lo Doc side – this involved its total abuse. I had numerous conversations with Tony Raggart of The Townsville Bulletin. I believe he got all the journalistic awards in Queensland for his many articles on the decline of Storm. He deserved them as his coverage was very comprehensive. Of course, many Storm investors were asset rich pensioners with very little or no income – in order to get paid Storm had to fiddle the books so to speak. This fraudulent activity was achieved via the new Lo Doc loan and its documentation. I am not exactly sure of the mechanics adopted (not being present) however, apart from pension income Storm added expected returns and probably other amounts (a real no no) so that declared income supported the loan request – in lots of cases I believe declared income exceeded $100K. This ensured loan approval for all the pensioners . I am sure that the job description pensioner would not have appeared on any loan application (perhaps investor/farmer) as it would have been declined automatically. Many loans were approved! The various banking organisations would obviously have benefited from the sheer volume of business written not knowing the level of rorting (definitely large scale). **Of course when Storm collapsed it all came out.** Still the lender commission generated in the ¾ year period prior to the GFC would have been staggering. From memory, a branch manager in North Ward, Townsville became a wealthy person - there would certainly have been others with increased earnings! As I see it the fraud was based on two things. Investors probably signed a blank Lo Doc Declaration. After that actual income would have been calculated by Storm (possibly an ex-bank employee) and they would have known what to insert too secure loan approval.

To this day, I am mystified as to how Cassimatus and a lot of other people didn't go to jail **for their criminal activity.**

While Storm was failing I remember seeing a news programme on TV with the owner of Storm in the foreground and a whole army of investors in the background in a large open space. The commentator's first question was a beauty and caused an enormous eruption from behind (the investors). The question was "did you tell all the investors that they could lose their house properties and farms when they signed up". Cassamatus said "yes" – hearing this, the investors went ballistic. Their indignation was palpable! Cassimatus was exposed as a big con and I know who I believe (the investors). Storm Financial was all about making **Cassamatus** wealthy. The GFC simply exposed the extent of his greed.

At some stage in the proceedings a firm of solicitors was appointed to help Storm investors and a class action followed. As with all things of this nature the poor old investor got done over and would have received small recompense for what happened to him. Many of the investors were old and lost everything.

The Lo Doc Form did not get amended until after the Storm Financial fiasco. It would certainly have been justified at the time. Actually, many of the wrong doings of that organisation would have been avoided had the ASIC amendments been done earlier.

I first met Keith Thomsen a little over 20 years ago. He used to stop by and have a yoghurt at my ice-cream shop in the K Mart Plaza opposite Stockland in Townsville. I had an ice-cream kiosk called Dal's and later changed its name to "Irresistibles". We always had a bit of a yarn and I quickly came to the view that he was clever and a shrewd businessman.

Anyway, this is a true account of Keith's dealings with Storm Financial. The company's early successes were highly publicised. Storm was literally the talk of the Town. I remember all the hype and everybody that had anything to invest was signing up. I am sure Keith was one of those that had plenty so he went and saw the owner of Storm – he later dropped in details of assets and all his financial interests including the Super plan. Cassimatus told him to leave everything with him and call back in a week. Keith called back and was told by Cassimatis that he had looked over everything and his recommendation was that Keith couldn't afford to muck around and it was all or nothing. Real slime-ball stuff! Maybe that's what alerted Keith. He looked Cassimatus in the eye and repeated "it's all or nothing eh". Oh well I guess it's nothing then! Keith picked up all his stuff and left the office.

I had no idea what Keith had but it must have been quite a bit. I dropped into his furniture shop in Ross River Road and the second hand business at the end of Boundary road near the Port a couple of times – it was the old style of bargaining over price with Keith (his family) and the businesses they operated. I think Linda and I bought a few things.

I admired Keith and particularly the way he handled Cassimatus (he was a lot smarter than that conman).

Keith was probably 25 years older than me. My only regret was not going to his funeral (as a mark of respect). Keith was an "icon" in the Townsville community and I am sure that it would have been attended by a lot of people.

The Lo Doc loan was pretty ordinary when it was first introduced however it's alive and well now. In my mind the ASIC amendments have made it bullet proof.

The Lo Doc Loan Facility is fully operational and completes the overall borrowing scenario. Any S/E person that needs money can now access it in any situation.

The Lo Doc Loan Facility combined with my wealth creating H/L is unbeatable.

It is important to realise that my home loan is assessed and approved by the same people that assess and approve conventional home loans. They must satisfy the same servicing and security criteria (and a first mortgage is always a prerequisite). A similar slightly repetitive comment is made further on in the "conclusion". The repetition is deliberate!

The real difference is that my home loan and a conventional loan are worlds apart – mine is incomparably better.

In my opinion a Conventional loan doesn't have much going for it. In my formative years as a finance broker I wrote a lot of those loans until I developed my own home loan system. At the same time, I didn't have much choice on what structure was acceptable - it had to be based on the conventional or traditional loan system, i.e. that was the only avenue for approval. There are lots of individual aggregators in this country with very similar or the same lending panels i.e. the major banks and a lot of other non-bank lenders are on the same panels. In many cases the only real difference is the software package used - broker attraction can range from different selling tools to different distribution methods. Is the broker part of a group that benefits from a different commission split? Is there an over-ride paid to the group? In all cases this determines who works for whom.

The aforementioned system also determines how the bulk of loans are distributed by finance brokers and others in this country. In addition, many of the banks and others, especially the Big 4 have their own mobile lending teams to increase their products in the market place. It points to the whole thing being a numbers game. Despite what they say and apart from some tweaking, they are all selling the same product (a Conventional home loan). I am talking about a massive amount of loans. The thing that worries me is - are Australians being hoodwinked on a large scale -there is a massive push to sell loans that are all basically the same. All of the different players are trying to say they have something different. I certainly don't agree with that. The difference between one **Conventional loan** and another is not worth talking about.

An individual broker must have accreditation with his own aggregator otherwise he doesn't have a job. Get into financial strife yourself and this opens "Pandora's box" - some aggregators won't employ you. You might have paid professional negligence insurance with no claims forever and know a personal and corporate balance sheet like the back of your hand. Suddenly you are un-employed despite years and years of training and experience. I suppose it would all depend on what the misdemeanor was. Some would deserve to be looking for another career some wouldn't.

In many ways these are strange times. I have been in finance all my life (over 50 years) and know I have something ground-breaking that needs to be passed on. I have a H/L system with many benefits - **it provides a mode of travelling in the financial world that makes a conventional loan look archaic**. You won't need a bank manager. You can do without his advice anyway. Is he friend or foe or wearing more than one hat? There is no way of knowing (refer earlier comment). You **will do a lot better yourself!** Be your own manager with investments that all **standalone**.

At my age, I am allowed to make a few observations regarding the industry I have spent a life-time in.

In recent years there has been no inflation (also no wages growth or very little). This explains why there has been limited interference by The Reserve Bank of Australia on interest rates. The "cash" rate effecting mortgages all over the country has simply remained the same. This is a good thing as nobody wants inflation especially the galloping variety (destroying economies all around the World in the recent past). I believe the practice of purchasing residential property by foreign Nationals (specifically people that do not live here) for capital appreciation **alone** i.e. for resale at a profit is unfair. These transactions do nothing for the economy and should not be permitted.

Australian Regulatory Authorities and Government Agencies have been doing their best to prevent this. Stable interest rates and interest only loans have enabled foreign nationals to bypass normal investment practice. I am talking about people that don't even live here and are still buying prime residential real estate. They have **no** tenant and only purchase to sell at a profit. This is not normal investment practice! It is however one of the reasons that normal Australians are being priced out of the market. Ever increasing prices (especially in Sydney and Melbourne) make it difficult for "Aussies" to own their own home or purchase investment properties.

There is more at issue with H/L's to Foreign Nationals. i.e. It is not as straight forward as it seems. If a Foreign National, perhaps a parent wants to purchase a residential property for their son or daughter to live in whilst attending university. This is entirely different to the speculative transaction mentioned previously. I am not opposed to this type of housing loan. Perhaps, the close scrutiny that all F/N transactions get is necessary after all.

My home loan system is all about Australians buying the family home and then buying investment properties after that. Everyone that uses my system will buy an investment property (likely more than one). This is far less prevalent with a conventional loan and there is a **huge** negative to watch out for (see next paragraph). It is my opinion that residential real estate should be for Australian citizens. They have a tenant, a normal investment loan to complete purchase and live in this country.

Use of a conventional housing loan implies use of equity and cross collateralising of securities - it also invokes the "all monies" clause that exists in every mortgage document. My H/L system **isolates each**

property transaction so that the borrower effectively avoids these clauses. They can certainly be detrimental to the unsuspecting borrower.

In my time I have probably been involved in all types of consumer lending: Hire purchase, leases, vehicle funding, home lending, personal loans, all types of Commercial funding and a few Foreign Currency Loans (FCL's). Customers are looking for a good deal no matter what the facility is. My system is far and away the best financial product I have ever seen - it is fair to the customer. A conventional loan is not! A home buyer with a mortgage shouldn't fall through the cracks especially if it is something out of the blue and not his fault. To lose your house involves the worst form of **ignominy**. A lot of resources and money goes down the Shute when a borrower falls over. I believe there are no winners in this situation and you never know -the borrower might be the victim of irresponsible lending.

My system would save the unfortunate borrower and transform the results of all the rest - it really is that good. It is not universal in this country, but I have always had a passion for it becoming so. As previously stated I haven't processed a conventional loan in 25 years.

I have it on good authority that one of the Major banks allows for trouble with 10 out of every 100 home loans approved. This statistic may be a bit harsh. I have since watered down my assessment (see below). Nethertheless, it sounds like the numbers game again. I would hate to be one of the ten - some would be destined to lose the family home and perhaps worse. I am sorry, but in many cases this outcome is simply not deserved. The borrowers in question originally qualified for a home loan and I have often wondered why they have failed or are failing. There would be the extreme cases where home ownership should be in jeopardy but not 1 in 10 or even 1 or 2 in 20. Whatever the case I have no doubts that the conventional loan is the culprit. That said the home loan facility backed by the mortgage document is pretty cut and dry i.e. pay-up or face the possibility of losing your house.

I think all of us fear change, but a lot of the time change is for the better. A conventional loan is just a big slog - paying off the loan every month or fortnightly for three decades. My home loan system offers a great deal more.

For the past 5 decades there has been no other home loan product. Now there is an alternative - **my**

home loan system. I have used this system individually as a finance broker for many years and haven't lodged a conventional loan application for twenty of those years. As stated some borrowers fall through the cracks with a conventional loan. My system avoids financial trouble (no mortgage stress) and it saves the casualties. It also gives everybody the opportunity of financial freedom. This includes those borrowers that are coping plus those that are well in advance with loan repayments.

Lately sales prices have eased a little i.e. in Sydney, Melbourne and other places. This is a good thing! Inflation is not the culprit this time but other economic factors. Hopefully this will be a turnoff for real estate buyers that don't live in Australia. **Hooray!**

I know that my system is incomparably better than any conventional loan in this country because I have been heavily involved with both. I have made a great deal of money using my own system and have enjoyed spectacular results passing it on to others over the last 25-30 years. Lots of things attest to this! I told you about my one disaster - a bit better than 1 arrears in every 10 loans with one of the Major banks that I know of (refer earlier comment).

Trust me and trust yourself - I have a foolproof method for getting ahead in life. It is a wealth creating home loan and for that reason alone is light years in front of what is currently available. You are fortunate if you are reading this E-Book (or book) as you will be able to take up my offer or at least fully investigate doing so. I have never had problems in the past and nobody will be twisting your arm. Let me say that one of my recent facilities is in Perth W.A. - a lovely fellow who I have never met (on his way to financial stability).

Let me say it's not a big decision! Lots of people spend a lot of money transferring from one conventional loan to another (a pretty futile exercise in my opinion as all of them are more or less the same). My home loan system settles the property and any refinance of an existing loan in the same way as a conventional loan (that's right exactly the same). The difference being that after settlement my system catapults borrowers to a better future. This simply doesn't happen with a conventional loan.

A Nationally based business entity and accounting company has looked at my financial product and said that it should go Australia wide. A franchise is certainly possible, or I might simply establish shops - I will shortly establish an Australia wide website in the name of "The Finance Specialists" this will get the ball rolling and determine what happens in the future.

After settlement, with my system your family home works for you while you live in it, pays off home loan debt in record time, gives great access to cash, buys investment houses, buys new cars, lose your job keep your house, turn your super into lots more money and importantly take control of your life and your finances. Out with the bank manager and you've got the job.

This is so important that I am going to highlight the whole paragraph -my system home loan has real structure. In other words, it gets the family loan and puts the correct machinery in place for future investment whereby each investment stands alone (is isolated). Investment should be confined to real estate as that is what it is designed for and the easiest. The machinery that I refer to is essential to investment success.

Please understand that whilst my facility is a wealth creating instrument after settlement, it is still a **RESIDENTIAL HOME LOAN**. It is approved by the same people that approve conventional loans. The offering

with my facility is financial stability and it is also much fairer on the borrower. Help establish this product in the market place, so all Australians can be better off.

If you are lucky and have a good paying job i.e. a higher income where leverage into the property market is a bit easier. We could be talking about a borrower with 5 or 6 investment properties with plans to have more. Of course, a bigger income than normal will always facilitate such activity. Unfortunately, users of conventional funding sources forget that banks and other lenders (the funders) have other priorities. The investment properties are acquired through either equity or stumping up the cash deposits for the purchases. In just about all cases this might involve a combination of both. However, it would definitely involve further funding from the **same** lender. Here in lies the problem! Funding from the same lender **automatically** invokes cross collateralising of securities as well as the all monies clause that is standard in all mortgage documentation that **you** the **borrower sign.** In the above instance, where a borrower owns several investment properties he is faced with many scenarios.

Do I sell some of the properties to restore liquidity (and perhaps reduce indebtedness elsewhere)? What properties should I sell? What properties are the worst effected? Do I buy more at the lower price? The difficulty is that the lender mightn't like your strategy. The borrower might have signed numerous mortgages but not necessarily on each investment property. The "all monies" clause in the original mortgage over the family home covers all the rest i.e. overall indebtedness. Effectively, all decisions are out of the borrower's hands – I don't think that this is necessarily a good thing.

Everybody is happy if property values go up but if they go down the banks money is also at stake. The banks strategy mightn't be the best however the difficulty is that the borrower is no longer calling all the shots. The real problem here is that each investment purchase is **not isolated from the one before or the family home**. The machinery for investment purchasing is put in place at the outset and **with my system every investment is isolated. I believe this aspect is paramount for the borrower**. Also, with my system the borrower makes all the decisions.

My loan system is easy to use and provides spectacular results. It is difficult to be pro-active with a conventional loan - it is impossible. It is a prerequisite with my system simply due to the many opportunities presented that can help achieve your own goals. After-all it is not just a home loan. All you need is awareness and familiarity and I will make sure you have both of those characteristics. A conventional loan serves its purpose and all you want to do is get rid of the commitment (the loan).

Everybody wants a home to live in and landlords tend to charge too much rent.

Affordability is a hot topic, but I think it's a bit overdone. My system can refinance the Sydney mansion or the $2M dollar unit and the owners can go on and make even more money. The important thing to realise that we are not talking about first home buyers (they don't start at the top). First home buyers can purchase further out in Brisbane, Sydney and Melbourne where saving the 10% deposit is **still** realistic (assuming 2 people work). Also, in many instances parents will chip in for their kids (10% can be $30,000 or for the above example it can be $400,000).

Young people must **first** get a foothold in the market. With my system you will have the cash to renovate and sell. You will also sell in a buyer's market and will soon be upgrading to the big house or unit in the inner suburbs.

You might also be selling an investment unit to make the up-grade. All of this is possible with my system.

I have shown my vulnerable side for a reason. I care! Australians should be purchasing their own homes to live in, in the knowledge that this can lead to a better life (and purchases in the future). This is not an elitist society and my system is all about maintaining Australians in the real estate market. I always harboured concerns about the plight of the borrower which lead to the creation of the loan system in the first place. **It gets rid of** the bank and the bank manager for all the right reasons and puts the borrower in control. There are no arrears or sell-ups – no mortgage stress. It also rockets the borrower towards financial independence and stability. You cannot have one without the other.

I repeat – I have always believed that the home loan borrower gets an ordinary deal in this country. And no choice! The facility that I designed almost 30 years ago is still relevant. It addresses the imbalance between lender and borrower. It is a wealth creation product after settlement and the lender has no arrears or sell-ups. I have cited my one case of loan arrears and do not attribute this to any fault in my system. Lenders should have designed it themselves – it is better for them and sensational for the borrower.

I have a H/L system that can lead to financial independence in a short period – trust yourself and give it a go (I will be).

I have been processing my home loans for many years. **My primary goal is to have my home loan system universally accepted – why not?** A Conventional loan has that status.

Let me say! My system is not a toy. It is much more than a conventional home loan. The filthy rich have plenty of money however having enough money is important to me (I believe it is essential). My system will make a rich man richer but more importantly it will **make the man in the street financially independent**.

We would all agree that access to credit is fundamental to purchase of the family home. Home buyers throughout history have had it – millions of Australians would not have got their own home without it. We also have some of the largest cities in the World (urban jungles spreading everywhere).

Actually it was on the news the other night. How the State Government was going to provide for the next raft of affordable housing in Brisbane? Look at Sydney

Harbour and the massive number of homes (big and small) before and after the Sydney Opera House. Imagine the prices of some of the real estate!

My system is all about making money out of your own home while you live in it.

There are a lot of people in the Sydney area that could be doing just that from Bondi and Coogee Beaches in the Western suburbs to Parramatta, on the North Shore through to Penrith and further out to Manly down to Palm Beach etc. There are beautiful houses everywhere! Brisbane is also huge with house prices increasing dramatically as you get closer to the City. Look at all the homes and water front units in the beautiful Sunshine and Gold Coast areas. Melbourne is also a sprawling giant with some of the best real estate in Australia. Look at Toorak, Hawthorn and Brighton! and what about the Peninsula? There is some really pricey real estate down that way and some great golf courses Sorrento, Portsea (the Ex PM's Beach). I must mention Barwon Heads Golf Course (it is so good and just outside of Geelong).

Incidentally, Melbourne would have the best collection of sand belt golf courses in the World. I am proud to say that the professional at Royal Melbourne was a friend of mine (he also introduced me to my lovely wife Linda). When I say making money out of the home I don't mean sitting in it and waiting for it to go up in value. I've already conceded that R/E can go up over time however, in the short-term its value can fluctuate widely (and go down).

The problem with the current system of home ownership is that it doesn't work for everybody. **It should!** Even some of the good one's fall through the cracks i.e. some that have saved the deposit and done everything right to qualify for loan assistance.

The Royal Commission into Financial institutions has exposed Corporations (especially The Big 4) for what they are. The Big Banks have different masters, different priorities – a different World where profitability/dividends are all that really matter. We all know that they do a veneer of advertising to attract home loan buyers etc. The reality is that they do their best to look after all their customers but Corporations like The Big 4 banks are also doing: commercial finance, all types of vehicle loans (novated leases, leases & hire purchase – sometimes via affiliates), personal loans, credit cards, professional packages for Doctors/Dentists including H/L discounts that you and I can't get (not elitist enough), home insurance, life insurance, personal guides to buying R/E and diverting customers into investments that **they** have funded themselves (I consider that a clear conflict of interest). Of course the banks administer all of their own facilities including credit cards (no doubt a massive job overall, especially for the majors). I think that they will continue to get bigger chasing the dollar and I can't see a leopard changing its spots.

In my first book I wrote about the old Bank of NSW (now Westpac). There was no Royal Commission into Financial institutions in those days – there certainly should have been given what happened. That bank foreclosed on a whole lot of farmers that had taken out Swiss Franc Loans (unhedged) on the bank's advice which was later shown to be totally incompetent. I don't think the farmers knew what they were doing but the Bank was no better. The farmers got together and appointed a lawyer firm to look after them – a class action ensued and was very successful in the long run. The wholesale selling up of farmers certainly scaled back a lot from that point on. The Bank of NSW was fully exposed in the end but was not in the least forthcoming. I believe full restitution followed but the bank was despised for more than the next decade for it's overbearing attitude. That bank survived and Westpac has certainly thrived since.

Are we seeing more of the same – there were no doubt some checks and balances in the old days. This is a worry in itself! Are The Majors at it again foreclosing on farmers and causing havoc. Going by the farmers the manner in which the banks are going about their work is anything but endearing. This time there is a Royal Commission into their actions and the farmer's woes are being listened too (as they should be). The Big Banks are not too subtle when they put people under. Lots of people are hearing about their tactics and are unimpressed – I think a bit of compassion is missing. Anyway it is fantastic how the farmers now have a voice. Long overdue in my opinion! Let's hope things are better in the future.

The question for me remains – do the mighty banks really care for the individual? I think not! If my information is correct in the H/L area they surely don't. If they are so big and clever why haven't they developed a H/L product that looks after the man in the street (not just a deal for Doctors/Dentists who shouldn't get anything special over everybody else anyway).

I have never voted for The Australian Labour Party! In my opinion their ideology of big government with bigger and bigger deficits (created by them) simply doesn't work. However to their credit, they have always been calling for a Royal Commission into the Big 4 Major Banks. And now we have one! The other night The Deputy PM was on a long running ABC programme, The 7.30 report. It is generally compered by Leigh Sales who does a great job (so does Laura Tingle). Anyway, he said what I am sure everybody knows and believes. The Major Banks act in their own interests and those of shareholders but really couldn't care less about the rest of us or the Aussie battler. I think untrustworthy is the word he used.

The Royal Commission certainly bears that out. The only positive that I will say about the Major Banks is that we live in a Capitalist Society in which monopolies are not condoned. On the other-hand **each is close to being** a **monopoly** plus they are government protected. In my opinion we have four Major Banks that are now trying to make all the decisions – an oligopoly i.e. The 4 Majors collectively acting together like a **monopoly**. Rumour has it that loans are harder to get in the major centres i.e. Sydney, Melbourne etc. My view has **always** been that The Reserve Bank is the governing body on interest rate movements (making its decisions on all sorts of economic data effecting Australia). I believe everybody accepts its role and The Reserve Bank's charter to act in the Countries best interest. **The Reserve Bank has no choice and its actions are a good thing.**

The Big 4 Banks make billions not millions and have **chosen self-interest and the mighty dollar (shareholders) over the man in the street.** The Majors are now putting up interest rates on residential home loans and making them harder to get. **This might swell the coffers initially but I think it is totally wrong. Let's hope it back-fires and they all lose custom!** There is no evidence of increased write-offs or anything else to justify their actions. One of The Major Banks suggested expenditures were being understated. Is this the reason loans are harder to get? In my mind this is absolute nonsense.

I have used my H/L system for the past 25/30 years with no sell-ups.

I have already discussed the expenditure issue and hope the public is not fooled. The Major Banks earn far too much and certainly don't need the additional revenue. Inflation and economic factors have traditionally played havoc with borrowers and residential house values. Now there is clear evidence that Major Banks are trying to manipulate a few things by themselves. **I hope they are**

stopped in their tracks as there are many other smaller lenders like First-mac, CUA , the mortgage division of AMP and a myriad of others that I believe can do a better job. I am a fan of First-mac partly because of their sponsorship of The Brisbane Broncos in the NRL. In my first book I wrote lots of pages on The Brisbane Broncos and The NQ Cowboys. I actually barrack for both Queensland teams. Many Legends of the game also play representative football (State of Origin). J.T. is a good example! Other legends relating to The Brisbane Broncos are also listed in this book.

Hopefully, First-mac and other lenders will realise what is happening and **not automatically follow suit on I/R's or anything else.** A borrower's loan application is already invasive – it doesn't have to be made more invasive. In the past, inflation has proven to be the hardest thing a borrower has to deal with i.e. it has a very **negative** effect on property values and I/R's. The Reserve Bank of Australia rules on rates **every month.** It has no choice in the matter – it must act as that is its charter. However, I believe The Major Banks are out of control in collectively increasing interest rates at the present time. This could result in a double whammy for H/L borrowers! Someone in the mortgage belt of Sydney with a reasonable size loan could be facing $400/500 extra per month. **The Major Banks don't allow for large rate increases at approval. Nobody else does either!** However it is not a burden for The Major Banks as it is all passed on to the borrower. **Why should they care!** The Majors may well argue that their servicing calculator allows for increases in interest rates (I can assure you the allowance is a pittance and not nearly enough given what they are doing).

There is also no reason for The Major Banks making H/L's loans harder to get. Property values have been falling recently and this should be a good time for all Australians to buy a home. I hope that there will be a mass exodus from the Big 4 Banks. The smaller banks will benefit from the increased custom and will do just as good a job (probably better).

Borrowers deserve a fair go and they are definitely not getting it – it's the current H/L system that needs overhauling.

My H/L system overcomes all these problems and is crying out for implementation universally.

I repeat The Major Banks have given scant reasons for making loans **harder to get.** If bad debts and write-offs were increasing perhaps there would be some logic to the move. I haven't heard anything that makes sense. If one of the Major Banks adopted my H/L system it would certainly improve their reputation over time. Shortly I will explain why!

There are supporters of the Big 4 Banks that maintain they do many good things in the community. The CBA sponsors the Cricket, ANZ sponsors the Tennis, NAB sponsors the AFL football via The NAB Cup and Westpac have the Rescue Helicopter Service. I am sure there are plenty of other worthwhile community services that they are involved in and they employ a lot of good people too. Earning Billions they can certainly afford to help out in other areas.

At the same time, it is important to realise that the gigantic revenues that the Big 4 Banks generate come in part from being tough on Commercial loans (and farm loans) and H/L 's alike. I also don't think there would be too many farmers that like Westpac given what the Royal Commission has disclosed. All of The Major Banks would have many areas of profit especially the lucrative insurance market on residential houses (with negligible claims).

This is probably a bit repetitive but it is important to demonstrate how little everybody gets with the existing conventional home loan. A perfect example is a car loan i.e. when you have no cash to buy the car yourself – you get the car and you also get a loan to repay (usually repayable monthly). This can be in the form of a vehicle or personal loan. The current home loan is exactly the same – the borrower gets the house and he also gets a loan to repay (a long-term repayment commitment over 3 decades). **Realise that it is only a loan!** The lender is in control irrespective of whether there is irresponsible lending after the original loan. This dreadful practice has already been discussed in detail but I must say it is rife amongst the Big 4 Banks. **However,** I do believe the real culprit here is the out-dated H/L that everybody is using. Here, the lenders trump card is its mortgage clauses keeping the so-called errant borrower in check. This punitive reminder is unnecessary - my system proves it **(I have had no sell-ups with my system in 30 years).** Current home loan borrowers must try and keep in advance with the loan i.e. by making fortnightly repayments reducing the loan term from 30 to 26 years or by paying extra. **Of course many can't get ahead and they are not protected at all. They should be!** What do they do if a financial crisis occurs? Unfortunately, the lack of protection is one of the biggest stumbling blocks in the current H/L (there are numerous other stumbling blocks but none of them exist in my system). H/L Borrowers still have loan terms of 30 or 26 years - what a joke! Why not clear your loan in a fraction of that time with my system.

With my H/L system the borrower gets the home and he also gets the loan. **This is where the similarity ends!**

I have talked about risk. Life itself is a risk! Getting out of bed is a risk! There will always be risk in Lending (and The Big 4 Banks do more of that than anybody else). However the current H/L poses an **unacceptable risk to the borrower. It must be changed! It must be fairer! My system ticks all the boxes.**
Additional benefits include:
- No mortgage stress – every H/L borrower must feel a little uncomfortable knowing that they **must provide for a long-term repayment commitment over 3 decades. My system relieves this strain completely.**
- Control switches to the borrower (where it should rightly be - after-all repaying the H/L is his responsibility). **Reliance on the local branch manager is a thing of the past (at the same time he will be writing more loans and providing more loan credits).**

- Clear H/L debt in record time (say 4 to 10 years).
- Use cash to purchase new cars and **change-over vehicles every ¾ years.**
- Invest in residential F/H property before and after retirement.
- Self Employed? Use business turnover to reduce the personal home loan interest you pay.
- Multiply your Superannuation payout 3/4 times.
- Enhance your livelihood and have a better standard of living.
- Many more borrower benefits which become evident after use.

As I have already said everybody is better off with my system (borrowers and lenders alike) – The Big 4 Banks then only need to determine who gets the CREDIT (I think the current qualifying rules for a H/L are hard enough i.e. most have to save a full 10% deposit plus a solicitor's fee and also keep a little aside for a rainy day).

I have already talked about irresponsible lending unfortunately it is rampart in The Big 4 Banks. In part this is due to the large number of branches that each Major Bank has.

This insidious affliction thrives in a branch network and all of The Majors have very large branch networks. Everything is fine when property values keep going up – the bank manager and the borrower are really happy and everything is rosy. However if property values do the reverse and go down or plummet quickly then a very different and nasty situation can occur. **Of course the big loser is the borrower (not the bank manager that made it all possible). What a joke!**

This sensational true storey is the worst case of Irresponsible lending I have ever seen. It actually defies belief! The whole thing appeared on the "60 minutes" TV programme about 4 years ago. Obviously buyers of residential property should be reasonably circumspect about what they do. However these two young people were caught out **big-time** and didn't deserve to have their lives destroyed. I'm pretty sure they had two young children. Anyway the camera's zoomed in on everything. The local branch (from one of The Major Banks) presided over the whole grubby incident by initiating a loan approval for a staggering $6.4M to purchase 20 investment properties. The couple's family home made up initial equity in the project. I believe some carpentry work was done on a few of the investment purchases after settlement. One investment property purchased for $1M was displayed on the programme. A local real estate agent charged with selling couldn't get $200k for it and it had no tenant. The other investment properties had also experienced a massive fall in value.

A scandalous funding by one of The Major Banks.

Naturally, the Major Bank did not appear on the show after-all how could it justify lending $6.4M s in a "boom or bust" district known for its volatility. The local branch had been in the district for 20 years and would be well aware of the vicious property cycles.

I believe The Major Bank signed this family's death warrant at approval.

Anyway it was all swept under the rug as only a major Bank can do. I was so incensed I wrote to the TV show but got no reply – rude in itself. I also got the disturbing impression that "60 minutes" had little sympathy for the couple who were out in the street with nothing. Perhaps all they were really after were the sensational headlines.

The Major Banks can be like doctors in that they bury their mistakes – this was one of those occasions.

I saw a recent "news" programme regarding a sell-up in Sydney by another of the Major Banks. The couple in question made the error of using equity in the family home. This appalling loss would never have happened had they been using my system. The male had a substantial **sole** income as a fly in fly out miner and had purchased 7 investment properties. The wife appeared on the news programme confirming that they were about to lose everything. Another disgraceful and depressing effort by a Major Bank!

A Major will never say "no" if it has the initial collateral to link each purchase. It knows that the "all monies" clause in any mortgage signed covers total indebtedness. **In my system every investment purchase is isolated so the borrower can zero in on the real reason for a default or declining performance and if necessary get rid of the property. If you borrow everything through the local bank then you can't dispose of anything. It's not your decision!**

I have commented on an almost identical case already. The difficulty could relate to: a bad investment, 2 investment properties not having tenants etc. Why? It is important to establish what has gone wrong. The borrower mightn't have purchased the property in first place if he had been privy to the valuation like the bank. Another dreadful case of **irresponsible lending by a Major Bank!**

These people would be going from strength to strength with my system (every investment isolated, no mortgage clauses to worry about, no mortgage stress, running their own show with a multitude of other benefits to ensure their future well-being).

Banks look after themselves and their lending margins and shell out the money and believe the borrower should handle the rest. This is the case with H/L's, commercial loans or anything else. The only thing I will say is that all relevant information should be shared with the borrower. After-all he has to pay the money back. Let's hope this happens in the future – if the borrower is privy to the valuation many poor investments could be avoided. In the current system only the lender sees the valuation. This is a real negative as the borrower should know about any defects so he can rectify them or alternatively not complete the purchase (find something else). A borrower can request a separate building report (at his expense) but should be able to confirm everything with his own bank at no cost.

Right now I don't believe there is a culture of co-operation between lender and borrower. I have been in finance all my life and believe this to be the case. You can only go by your own experiences.

I was not going to talk about my own financial downfall again (I lost millions in real estate) but I will. Whilst I made mistakes with my brother these were understandable. **He was my brother and we were close all our lives except for the last few years. The GFC followed and made it difficult to sell anything. I am a clever person (and had a brilliant father) and don't say any of that boastfully. I have had a dreadful time in the past 8 years. .** At a time when I needed help from the Major Bank that I was dealing with, I got none. I had also sent them a considerable amount of good business. They made me feel like an outsider and a criminal. I've had a lot of time to reflect on what happened and they had a bigger hand than anyone else in me falling over.

I have certainly done my share of bank bashing and there is more to follow – in addition to what the Royal Commission has dredged up. At the same time I lay my own financial demise firmly at the feet of a Major Bank – see previous paragraph.

Obviously, if you are building a large factory or purchasing a residential home to live in the ability to access **credit** is critical. Not to many can do it on their own! Banks (and the Majors) have historically been the ones to cover this requirement and this will not change. I believe what **must** change is the spirit of co-operation between lender and borrower.

I will be doing a bit of a backflip on the Banks (and The Majors) in my final remarks. This will be on the basis of a **recommendation for change.**

The fact is I have a H/L product that looks after people that earn a lot more than the rest of us, including Doctors/Dentists and professional athletes etc. It is a million times better than what any bank has to offer.

One thing that I haven't discussed elsewhere in this book is the reverse mortgage for older Australians. My system leads to the same people making much more before and after retirement. Generally a reverse mortgage is given to people that have had a tough life under the current system. They may have put part of their Super into the house to clear the mortgage and spent the rest i.e. to cover cost of living increases etc.

In many cases their only asset is the house. They have no income to repay so a reverse mortgage is arranged and hopefully is enough to get through. At some stage the house is sold, the banks first mortgage cleared with remaining funds going to the family estate. I believe the reverse mortgage is to be avoided and not a good product.

My product is totally superior and leaves people with so much more at the end of their lives – dignity is an important thing at that time.

I have heard a rumour that CBA is dropping the reverse mortgage from its H/L facilities –certainly no loss in my opinion.

My financial product satisfies the two critical areas that a borrower must have if he is to make a go of it i.e. **access to credit and taking control** . A guy that runs a business might consult others but he is the Boss and makes all the decisions. Borrowing money for the purchase of the family home is only one of the big life decisions that we all have to make. Why not use a H/L where you make the decisions (not the bank). **What is currently available doesn't allow that.**

You don't have to be discerning to realise that there is a lot more at stake than this.

If you want to change your life for the better! Make all the decisions! Help yourself and your family! Have a much better way of life! Then read this book and know that you can make it happen. There isn't a system for life but I know that good decision making is part of the answer. If you make a bad decision you soon know about it. I've made plenty of them and been stuck with the results (and decisions have never been reversible for me). I believe that learning how to avoid bad decisions in life is the big lesson that we all have to learn.

My H/L system is you making all the decisions – even though I have had one scare with a borrower that broke all the rules (and a criminal) there was no confirmation of his downfall i.e. in 25-30 years. The banks allow for people falling over all the time (losing the house and everything else).

This is a repeat of the numbers game and nobody wants to be one of those numbers (or one of the statistics). **There is now an alternative that has no downside for borrowers and is many, many, many times better than what is available.**

It will also teach you to be a better decision maker (being proactive is part of the lesson).

I've talked about lots of things and the **need** to be pro-active. This is because there are so many benefits to be obtained including those that can be achieved by combining benefits (just after the bullet point section in chapter 2 this is discussed in detail). **The most important thing is to pursue what you really want.** Actually, I probably wasn't proactive enough myself when I got into financial trouble.

I don't know if that was the thing that was missing but I do know that fear took over. **Fear** is a very negative emotion no matter how you look at it. Certainly, nothing good comes from feeling fearful – in my mind I was only trying to help my brother. I should have been thinking about my own family (and wife) and not my own decline.

Before my brother got really sick with cancer I was working on resurrecting one of his old companies. He had a clear credit rating at the time. Amazing in itself! I had intended that this company would be the recipient of one of my systems. It would have been, had he not double-crossed me just before everything was finalised.

I could never understand why he did this. We were good friends (unfortunately, I was the only one thinking along those lines at that time) and he would have made heaps of money. I guess the big lesson for me was – row your own boat.

A good friend of mine has a large family of brothers and sisters but he is the only one that is wealthy. He is also a generous bloke but has taught me that there has to be limits to any generosity i.e. you only back a horse with what you are prepared to **lose.** I backed my brother and lost the lot – a harsh penalty but certainly my own fault.

I now believe that you have to run your own race with as much focus as you can muster. I have always believed that you live and die by the decisions you make – my two sons are good decision makers. It is also important to know when to cut your losses. I retired to the Sunshine Coast just out of Brisbane and would still be there if I had followed that principle myself.

Having said the above I am motivated and need to get my life back and that of my wife's. I have always believed that you can achieve anything you really want i.e. think and grow rich just like the book. You attract what you think about. If you consistently think that you will be in a car accident then it is no coincidence when it happens. This is a very negative example but the positive side of thinking/visualising (consistently) of things you want is many times **more powerful than any negative force.**

My wealth creating home loan provides a variety of outcomes – using it properly you can improve your life situation and attain financial independence. Everybody is different but people from all walks of life can create a freedom that they have never had before. There was a weakness with my brother that I should have acknowledged. **I really don't how I stuffed up, but I did.**

Life itself is a risk! Those human beings that take no risks (apart from being bored) have an uneventful life. In my opinion they die ignominiously and are not missed even by their family. A famous anonymous quote is appropriate and goes as follows "but risk we must because the greatest hazard in life is to risk nothing". The well-known and inimitable Hollywood performer Danny Kaye also said "Life is a great big canvas and you should throw all the paint on it that you can". We should all heed those very wise words.

The system that I lucked onto (my own) is infallible. You and I aren't but we can aspire to make good decisions. One of those is to look after YOUR family (my mistake).

After use I am sure you will come to think my home loan is infallible (and far less risk than a normal loan). In fact I have spent a life-time taking all the risk out of it.

All Australians should embrace my wealth creating home loan – it is a million times better than what is available.

Remember the borrower pays NO commission. I am a fully accredited finance guy with all the required knowledge.

This is not a long book but I believe the message is clear none the less. I have a "tried and true" home loan system that is far better for the borrower in so many ways (and it is fully demonstrated here). Its universal acceptance and use throughout Australia is the objective of this book.

I wasn't going to attack traditional loans but there really is no alternative. – my product is **totally superior.** The dedication in this book is un-equivocal and should be read by everyone. For too many decades there has been no choice! **Now there is one!** In many instances the current H/L facility is a brutal and inflexible facility. The borrower gets the house and a long-term repayment commitment over 3 decades. **And that's all he gets!** This is OK for some but a lot of good borrowers fall through the cracks. Good people that have struggled raising kids and at the same time saved both the deposit (normally 10%) and conveyancing costs. **They don't deserve to lose everything. It really is the Australian dream to buy your own house. Home ownership is in our culture** like The Sydney Harbour Bridge or The Opera House. Both of those magnificent landmarks and many others were commissioned by Australians. **They deserve the best in housing!**

Depending on the location, a 10% deposit for a house can vary a lot from place to place i.e. a range of say $25 to $60K. Then add in solicitor's costs plus a little extra to cover the unexpected. A sizeable investment for any home buyer! What- ever you do never give up on owning a house (renting is more invasive and is dead money in most instances). Some parents are sub-dividing their properties so that their kids remain close and have a home of their own. I think that the recent decline in house values is a good thing especially for the army of young Australians that still aspire to home ownership. **Hope is the driving force and home ownership is within all our grasps. Heck, I don't own for the first time in my life.** I can tell you paying rent is no fun when the priority is to be an owner again. **I am 72 and haven't given up – make sure you don't.**

I have already discussed affordability. Even in the big centres of Brisbane, Sydney and Melbourne houses are affordable. Young Australians can start in the outer suburbs where the deposit is significantly less than closer in. Houses in Hobart, Adelaide, outer Perth and some of the regional cities like Geelong, Newcastle, Freemantle, Bundaberg, Townsville and lots of others will be more affordable. The smaller centres will always be a bit cheaper and further price falls are expected.

As far as I am concerned the biggest problem is the current home loan facility. It is simply not doing the job well enough. Often equity in the family home is the only thing accessible. That's not the banks fault! Unfortunately, this can be disastrous for new investors. New property investors should be safe in thinking purchase of an investment property is a good thing. Generally this is the case but sometimes it isn't. I have already discussed this and other risks – part of the trouble is that equity in the family home can vanish overnight. **In some circumstances losing the lot is a possibility. This is an unacceptable outcome for a person that owns their own home and simply wants to invest further in real estate.** In my opinion a conventional loan is a lottery for borrowers – **good for some and bad for others.** After 50 years it has lost relevance and should be used less and only where there is less risk to the borrower. **This is the real problem with the current H/L!** There are too many transactions with an unacceptable level of risk for the borrower.

I would like to emphasise the following:

- A Nationally based Accounting and Business Equity Firm has seen my H/L system and has said it should go Australia wide.
- My H/L system is "tried and true" over the last 30 years - before this I processed conventional home loans. I repeat my system will make a rich man richer and the man in the street financially independent.

- The existing lender bias is reversed with my system – its removal is a good thing and **delivers a much better outcome for lenders and borrowers alike.** A lender's income is more stable and there are no sell-ups. Lenders will also benefit from Australians buying a lot more investment properties than they do now. I actually believe bankers are trying to help but are hindered by shortcomings in the standard H/L.

Purchase of the family home is not financed on **equity** nor is any investment house or unit. Using **equity** is where an irresponsible lender can later rely on its mortgage document for recovery – all of this is avoided with my system.

- My system has the potential to dominate for decades to come. **Essentially because everybody is better off!**

If bankers especially the Big 4 adopt my product I believe their poor reputation will recover despite The Royal Commission. My product is a home loan just like any other – take the "wealth" word out of equation (or the heading) if that makes you more comfortable.

Banks will be better off and be able to concentrate more on what they do best i.e. **providing credit to borrowers.**

Bank bashing has become fashionable during the Royal Commission. However, banks are an essential part of any Capitalist Economy. I believe the banks have been caught out but they do accomplish many good things in the community. Perhaps, we should acknowledge the good and not be so quick to criticise the not so good. In recent times the banks have embraced the current H/L facility but they do many other things as I have already pointed out. My criticism is restricted to the current H/L due to the fact that it is punitive on borrowers. Mine isn't!

Many people in the community are distrustful of banks and have a **fear** of borrowing from them. I am talking about people with experience! People with a much greater chance of success who are letting opportunities go because they are weary of banks. This is not how it should be.

My home loan system will do away with this and needs to be **implemented universally** - banks can then pass on greater benefits to borrowers.

Making the H/L harder to get is definitely not the way to go – that will be worse for the borrower (and totally unnecessary).

FINAL MESSAGE

Decades ago, I read the immortal classic "A Tale of Two Cities" by Charles Dickens. This was my second reading of the book. In my opinion the author had a great talent similar to that of Shakespeare himself. This fictional story was written about the French Revolution. The Monarchy of that country were all beheaded. The book ends with a very famous quote. A quote that reveals an extraordinary act of courage! It (the quote) goes as follows "It is a far better thing that I now do than I have ever done, it is a far better rest that I go to than I have ever known". To me this signifies a couple of things -without doubt, an extraordinary act of courage. Perhaps the Australian home-buyer displays something similar, perhaps not an extraordinary act of courage but courage nonetheless.

More than 3 decades ago I had a deep conviction that there was something seriously amiss with the **home loan.** A home loan that hasn't changed in the last 70 years and one that probably dates back to the days of early settlement. It helps get the house and that's all (doesn't help keep it).

Australia has a culture of home ownership like no other country on earth. There are millions of houses in Australia perhaps 30/40 million with mortgages.

Men and women everywhere bite the bullet and take out a H/L. They stump up the deposit, meet the solicitor's conveyancing cost and enter into a long-term repayment commitment over 3 decades or longer. **This is undeniably an act of courage!** I am sure that many of them don't realise what is involved. The lucky ones survive and there are those that are successful in other areas. Many though are not so lucky. The current H/L doesn't have any frills. It is a brutal facility that can see the family home lost overnight in a variety of ways. Some H/L borrowers will also never know that their loss might have been due to irresponsible lending (equity lending) – **the lender's domain**. Health issues, sudden job loss, death of a spouse, children with health difficulties are nearly always outside the control of the home buyer. A H/L is a long term repayment commitment and none of us are privy to future events.

Part of the problem is that The Major Banks (Westpac was the first) and The National News all zeroed in on the massive number of H/L defaults already underway in the Sydney/Melbourne markets i.e. difficulties with the current home loan. The Royal Commission into the workings of financial institutions was up and running at that time. It changed the Credit Code and identified many terrible and unsavoury practices. Despite this I am sceptical that this will provide greater protection for H/L borrowers. In fact I am very sceptical! Lenders and borrowers have very different and conflicting interests.

A conventional H/L is just a loan. Low interest rates are attractive now and the economic prediction into the future is that they will stay low (with low inflation). This is still a transitory phase! I remember when H/L interest rates exceeded 15% per annum. **People should remember that a prediction is just that – there are no guarantees.** I signed up a H/L many years ago where the borrower fixed a major portion of his loan at 8.5%pa in anticipation of rates going still higher. I/R's did the reverse and he paid 3% more for 3 years. Needless to say he blamed me anyway.

There are many aspects to my system – life changing aspects that you will **never get with a loan.**

The National News has predicted that there will be 60,000 H/L defaults in Sydney and Melbourne this financial year (2019). This is a damming statistic!

This is not over time and does not include the rest of Australia. **With my system I have not had a reportable loss in 30/35 years.**

A recent news survey said that the two greatest quandaries in life for human beings (not just Australians) was (1) what livelihood and income will there be for me? & (2) who will pay the mortgage?

A family home shouldn't be the obstacle that it is. For many the current H/L is just that – a big obstacle. Getting the first family home (or the 2ND or 3RD) should be a wonderful event. Unfortunately, the risk of loss is ever present under the current system. Many try to deny this but the statistics are correct and accurate. The number of good people that are losing their houses in Sydney and Melbourne is astounding – a tale of misery actually. The situation is so bad that I will quote one example from the news. Years ago, a fellow purchased a family home for himself and his wife in French's Forest – the asking price was $500K. He put in $250,000 in cash and borrowed the rest (a H/L). He loved the place and when he purchased it, said to himself I will live here forever. Unfortunately, the scenario that unfolded was something entirely different (a nightmare). Due to ill health and two serious operations (one was putting a stent in his arteries to avoid a heart attack) he could not work for an extended period. The house value went up but so did the H/L - a million dollars owing and the loan is 30 days in arrears. **This is a heart-breaking situation!** This person and his wife have seen a financial adviser who has told them their only option is to sell. When they do they will be out on the street with nothing and no chance of getting another house. **This is the worst possible outcome.** I could cry! This person would have no H/L debt with my system.

In this country, if you experience financial difficulty that in itself is a real impediment to getting another H/L even if you have a cash deposit. It is wrong but there is almost no opportunity or second chance given. My H/L avoids the financial difficulty in the first place.

I strongly believe that "who pays the mortgage" is still a big problem because of the current home loan. **Replace the H/L with my system and the problem disappears along with financial difficulty.**

I believe the borrowers main concern is – will I retain my family home? And will I kick on in life and be better off?

Expectations are low but I attribute this entirely to the current H/L (after-all it has been in for 70 years). **My H/L ensures a borrower will retain the family home and become financially independent (remember my system is "tried and true" over decades without a default).** These aspects are the cornerstone of my system – a system that provides so much more.

In this modern world where accurate news is really in your face the Australian public deserves better. My system H/L is 12 million times better than what is available.

Give it a go! One day my system will be universal. I made all my money from it previously.

The purchase of the family home is still an act of courage with my system – a selfless act by the borrower. It is also a journey where the borrower is the driver and his destination is financial independence. It is also a safe journey and one that is not at present!

SUMMARY

If you have an existing home loan or are purchasing a residential house anywhere in australia - in all cases use my system. Read this section again and again until the message sinks in - my home loan gives you so much more. My system is also just a home loan but it is the right one, that delivers the right outcomes for the borrower.

I often look at the reverse cover of this book and believe there is a big responsibility on me to pass on details of my loan system. A system that is so much better than what is available! Australians will be better off and experience a financial freedom that they have never known. We are all different and will arrive at financial independence at different times but we can all get there with my system. Remember I am a long-term financial person with an Australian Credit Licence and I designed this thing.

Shacka

www.ingramcontent.com/pod-product-compliance
Ingram Content Group UK Ltd.
Pitfield, Milton Keynes, MK11 3LW, UK
UKHW021300180426
11947UKWH00015B/944